D0763990

Praise for *Inside the Soul of Islam*:

'One of the most important books to have been written and a monumental step towards giving the wisdom teachings of Islam their rightful place in the self-help genre. Mamoon successfully relays across the essence of the soul and universality of Islamic wisdom through a personalized yet truthful account of his physical and spiritual journey.'

– Sami Yusuf, globally bestselling musician, composer, and singer-songwriter

'An excellent, authentic way of describing the beauty of Islam in the day-to-day life of a Muslim. Mamoon's personal story makes this an easy read for anyone who wants a realistic introduction to the spiritual aspect of Islam. I hope and pray that every seeker of the truth, especially those who live in the Western world, will read this book.'

– Sheikh Ahmed Babikir, Islamic scholar, imam, and spiritual guide; founder of Rumi's Cave and Ulfa Aid

'If you've ever wondered how people can believe in a religion that is so often used to justify terrorism and hate, this shockingly wise, deeply personal, and surprisingly humorous book will take you "behind the words" and connect you to the very heart of Islam – your own unconquerable soul.'

– Michael Neill, bestselling author of *The Inside-Out Revolution* and *The Space Within*

'Mamoon is one of the most inspiring, uplifting, and transformational coaches I know. His teachings bring light and love to all our lives and his message has the power to bring peace to the world.'

– Christian Mickelsen, bestselling author of *Abundance Unleashed*

'Mamoon has the gift of taking the beautiful, spiritual teachings of Islam and can personalize them in a way that makes it both universal and easily accessible. This book is a joy to read and gives a refreshing take on Islamic spirituality.'

– Isam Bachiri, singer-songwriter for multi-award winning hip-hop group Outlandish

'Mamoon has a deep, profound understanding of how the mind works which casts a new light on one of the world's most controversial religious traditions.'

– Jamie Smart, author of the *Sunday Times* bestseller *Results: Think Less, Achieve More*

'*Inside the Soul of Islam* invites everyone – of all faiths – to surrender to Universal Love, and to choose love over fear. Mamoon Yusaf's beautiful book shows us how to do this.'

– Robert Holden, author of *Loveability* and *Shift Happens!*

'An excellent introduction to the essential values of Islam written by a sincere seeker of wisdom, who has a deep understanding of the human mind. This book offers clarity in a time where there is much confusion and misunderstanding surrounding Islam.'

– Shaykh Sharif H. Banna, Advisory Board Member of the Centre for Islamic Legislation and Ethics

'This book insightfully grasps how the biggest problem facing humanity is not religion or politics, but a misunderstanding about how the mind works. To fix the psychological puzzle the world is in we do not go into the puzzle. Because the psychological puzzle is the mess. The answer, *Inside the Soul of Islam*, is the answer within us all.'

– Keith Blevens PhD, co-founder of the Three Principles Paradigm

Inside *the* Soul *of* Islam

Inside *the* Soul *of* Islam

A UNIQUE VIEW INTO THE
LOVE, BEAUTY AND WISDOM OF ISLAM FOR
SPIRITUAL SEEKERS OF ALL FAITHS

MAMOON
YUSAF

HAY HOUSE
Carlsbad, California • New York City • London
Sydney • Johannesburg • Vancouver • New Delhi

Published and distributed in the United States by: Hay House, Inc.: www.hayhouse.com® • ***Published and distributed in Australia by:*** Hay House Australia Pty. Ltd.: www.hayhouse.com.au • ***Published and distributed in the United Kingdom by:*** Hay House UK, Ltd.: www.hayhouse.co.uk • ***Published and distributed in the Republic of South Africa by:*** Hay House SA (Pty), Ltd.: www.hayhouse.co.za • ***Distributed in Canada by:*** Raincoast Books: www.raincoast.com • ***Published in India by:*** Hay House Publishers India: www.hayhouse.co.in

Cover design: Ploy Siripant • *Interior design:* Leanne Siu Anastasi
Interior images (pp. 1, 71): Oktora, Shutterstock • *Indexer:* Dave Cradduck

Library of Congress Control Number: 2017948502

Hardcover ISBN: 978-1-4019-5372-0

10 9 8 7 6 5 4 3 2 1
1st edition, November 2017

Printed in the United States of America

Dedicated to my Beloved.

May the peace, love, and blessings of Allah be upon him.

Contents

Introduction

As an intelligent and conscientious global citizen, you've probably noticed that in the last 20 years the world seems to have gone a little 'crazy' when it comes to Islam. We could put this down to political actors, misguided fundamentalists, sloppy or even agenda-driven media coverage, the inability of Muslim communities to effectively communicate the teachings of Islam, or an all-out apocalyptic conspiracy.

To whatever cause we attribute today's attitudes toward Islam, the truth is that for many in the West, it's become virtually impossible not to believe some of the negative – and more importantly, untrue – things being said about the religion.

You, however, have been conscientious enough to pick up this book, which suggests that somewhere in the depths of your soul, you intuitively understand that something's amiss in the picture being presented to you. In fact, the more blatantly Islam and its adherents are portrayed as evil, bloodthirsty 'threats' to Western civilization, the more astonishing it becomes when you actually take a minute to talk to one of us. Your Muslim doctor, neighbor, or work colleague simply doesn't fit the caricature.

When I was at school, some 20 years ago, *no one* believed Islam was a dangerous or violent faith. Today, though, I'm considered controversial for suggesting that it *remains* a religion of peace. There's a tragic irony here: even while Islam appears to be the most hated religion in the USA, that country's bestselling poet is Rumi, the classical Muslim scholar and spiritual master. We *must* be missing something here.

'I am nothing but dust on the path of
Muhammad, the Chosen One.'

Rumi

'The Ben Affleck Problem'

Logic dictates that Muslims can't all be bad people, and that a faith with around 1.5 billion followers worldwide (a quarter of the global population) can't be based on evil teachings. So, when the topic of Islam and Muslims comes up during coffee breaks at work, or when you're having a night out with your friends, you might choose to stick up for your Muslim brothers and sisters – and may Allah, the Most Loving, bless you for it. However, if you do so, my guess is that you'll soon run into what I call the 'Ben Affleck Problem.'

In 2014, the American actor Ben Affleck became involved in a heated discussion about Islam while appearing on a US TV talk show. The show's host and the other guests argued that Islam is obviously a big problem today – given all the true-sounding, yet false, claims being made about it.

As a guy who's smart enough to realize that people are being duped into believing things that can't *possibly* be true about an entire religion, Affleck became visibly annoyed by their comments. That was quite surprising to many Muslim viewers because we've become almost completely desensitized to this kind of negative talk about Islam.

Affleck was frustrated that a community that had no one present to speak up for them was receiving so much hate – there were, of course, no Muslim guests on the show – so *he* did the talking. 'How about the more than one billion people who aren't fanatical, who don't punch women, who just want to go to school, eat some sandwiches, and pray five times a day?!' he exclaimed.

As I watched a video of the show[1] – which went viral on YouTube and has probably been seen by more Muslims worldwide than any other group – I looked into Ben Affleck's eyes and had two realizations. Firstly, like millions of other young Muslims, I thought: *Woah… this guy really could pull off Batman*. Secondly I thought: *We've crossed a threshold; the dramatic lack of understanding between Westerners and Muslims has now reached a dangerous tipping point.*

None of us wanted this to happen, but it has. For Western Muslims, this is the worst-case, nightmare scenario that we feared would emerge after 9/11: one in which open-minded liberals who'd normally stand up against racism and bigotry have turned against the Muslim community and, even worse, the religion we love so dearly.

Although Mr. Affleck was smart enough to know that the other guests on that TV show were not 'the official interpreters of the doctrine of Islam,' he was going on his faith and intuition that Islam isn't the 'mother lode of bad ideas' as was being claimed, and that the arguments put forward couldn't possibly be representative of a quarter of the world's population.

And therein lies the 'Ben Affleck Problem.' Like most Westerners who want to believe that at its core, Islam is a good religion, Mr. Affleck, may Allah bless him, was going on his *faith* that Islam teaches good stuff. However, it was not concrete *knowledge* of what it actually does teach.

No faith required

The good news is that we no longer need to depend entirely on hope or faith, because in this book is something much stronger and more sturdy that can bring our hearts together, and offer more peace of mind to us all when it comes to Islam: *sound knowledge.*

So many people believe that the values of Islam are fundamentally incompatible with the values of the West, but if we ask them what the values of Islam *are*, they draw a blank. Some are convinced that Islam is a violent religion, instead of one based on love and peace, like other world faiths.

But it soon becomes apparent that they're unaware of even the most basic teachings of the Prophet Muhammad, peace and blessings upon him. Many hear and use Arabic terms such as *jihad* and *Shariah* – believing that they're bad things – yet they wouldn't be able to tell you accurately what those words *mean*. (You'll discover their true meaning later in the book.)

At the same time, people are becoming increasingly aware that Muslims are very deeply devoted to Islam, and for many of them, this is quite mysterious, especially in an age when religion is regarded as antiquated.

Why did that bearded African-American gentleman pull out a rug in the middle of New York City and start praying, completely unfazed by the noise and lights around him? Why is it that my father – who isn't considered religious by the community and doesn't even think of himself as religious – still prays five times a day, every single day, without fail?

How do Muslims have the discipline to fast from dawn to dusk for an entire month every year? Why is it that the local mosque is absolutely packed every Friday – to the point where it creates parking problems for the rest of the community – when the numbers at most Christian church services in the West are dwindling? (By the way, I don't believe in collective guilt – I think that everyone is responsible only for what they do themselves – but in this instance, I sincerely apologize on behalf of the entire Muslim community for the parking problems.)

What is this mysterious and almost magnetic power that Islam has, and what do all these people see in it? Could there be a deeper way for us to understand the religion, and even be touched by it, such that it enhances our lives – irrespective of our beliefs and background? I believe that there is.

What this book is about

In this book I aim to answer all these questions and more. I've focused on three specific objectives:

1. Firstly, within Islam there's a massive body of knowledge that most Muslims are brought up with and almost all non-Muslims are completely unaware of. These are the essential values on which the religion is based. By the end of this book, you'll know more about the values, ethics, and basic teachings of Islam than the vast majority of the non-Muslim population.

2. However, if we stopped there, this book would be about only the 'body' of Islam, and not its 'soul.' I want to go

deeper with you. So my objective is to share with you 'the Inside-Out Paradigm' – a psychological understanding that can act as a catalyst on the teachings of Islam, and lead to spiritual evolution in anyone, regardless of their beliefs, religion, or background.

This psychological understanding has enabled me to use the Quran as a divine 'personal development manual,' and a source of healing. It's given me a much deeper respect and reverence for my own faith, and all other religions and spiritual traditions, too. I'll explain in detail how it works later in the book, but for now, just be aware that our aim is to explore the spiritual teachings of Islam alongside an approach to psychology that will make them relevant to your life.

3. Along the way, I hope to surprise and delight you as we take a fresh look at some of the controversial 'hot-button' topics surrounding the presence of Islam in the West. You'll quickly see how many of these issues are rendered obsolete, and can even look quite comical, when we view them with a slightly deeper and more grounded understanding of the religion.

I want to show you the love, beauty, and spiritual depth of Islam in which I'm immersed. I want you to know what the Prophet Muhammad, may the peace and blessings of God be upon him, gifted us, and in such a way that you can be touched by it too. I want to open your heart to the depth of the teachings of Islam – including those that never make the headlines because love, joy, and transcendence are not considered newsworthy.

My hope is that in taking this approach, our collective consciousness will be raised, and as a result, more understanding and love will grow between us, by Allah's grace.

I can see why, at this particular point in history, some people may dislike the image and the superficialities associated with Islam. And I'm equally certain that anyone who's blessed with even the slightest glimpse into the 'Soul of Islam,' will be so deeply touched by it, that they can't help but fall in love with it. In a way, you can think of this book as a love letter from deep within the Soul of Islam, hoping to reach the depths of your soul.

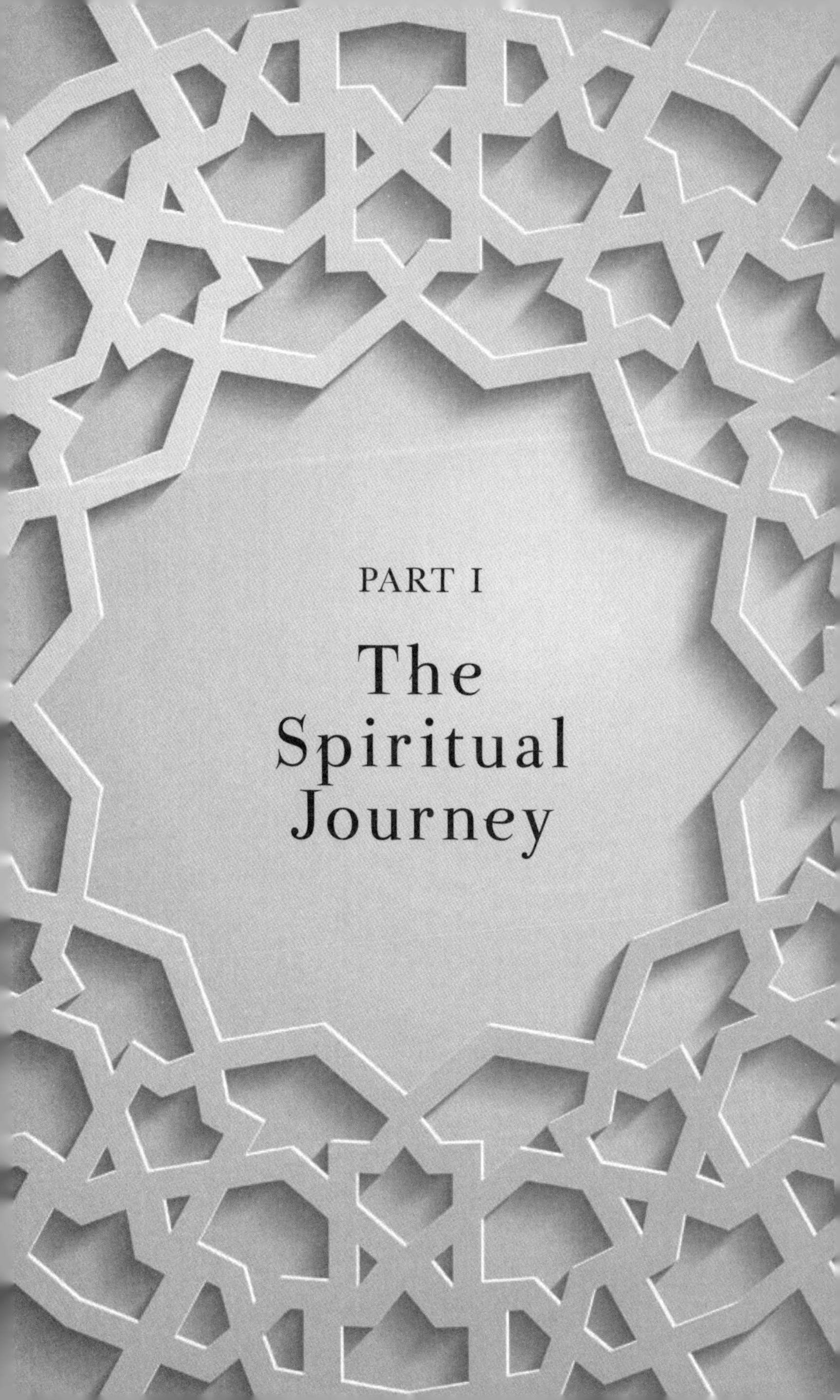

PART I

The Spiritual Journey

CHAPTER 1

What Is the Soul of Islam?

'Islam can be summarized in three sentences:
Be with the Creator, without creation.
Be with creation, without ego.
Wish for others what you wish for yourself.'

Shaykh Zakariya al-Sidiqqui

Let's begin with a story. Some people think that what follows is a myth, but I believe it to be absolutely, literally true.

The beautiful stranger

Long ago, in a land far, far away, a group of men were enjoying a gathering in a simple house located in the middle of the desert.

Although you wouldn't have known it by looking at him, due to his humility, one of the gentlemen seated on the floor of the house was very well known in the region for his impeccable character, trustworthiness, and kindness. Despite these qualities, he'd been accused of disrupting public order; theirs was a tribal society so corrupt and immoral that a good man couldn't help but do so. So, although the gentleman was loved by those who knew him well, he was a wanted man.

Suddenly, as if from nowhere, into the house walked a magnanimous figure of such stature and sublime beauty that no one in the room could take their eyes off him. The men were struck with awe at the sight of this stranger, who had jet-black hair and wore pristine white clothes. There was nothing particularly impressive about the latter, apart from the fact that they were deep in the desert, and there was no sand on the man, nor any signs of travel.

The beautiful stranger walked over to the kind, trustworthy man and sat down directly in front of him, such that their knees were touching. Although the men in the gathering were ready and willing to give their lives to protect the kind, wanted man, shockingly, none of them found themselves able to get up and respond to the stranger's actions. They were literally stunned by the presence of the man.

The beautiful stranger put his hands on the gentleman's knees and said: 'Muhammad, tell me what Islam is.' Muhammad, peace and blessings upon him, replied:

'Islam is to testify that there is no deity except Allah and that Muhammad is his messenger, to perform the prayer, to give the purifying charity, to fast during Ramadan, and to perform Hajj to the House, if you are able to do so.'

The stranger replied: 'You have spoken the truth.'

The men in the gathering were astonished. Who did this person think he was, and who was he to tell the Prophet Muhammad, peace and blessings upon him, that he was correct?!

The stranger then said: 'Tell me what faith is.'

The Messenger of Allah, peace and blessings upon him, replied: *'It is that you believe in Allah, His angels, His books, His Messengers, in the Last Day, and in the Divine Decree, both the good and evil of it.'*

Again, the beautiful stranger said, 'You have spoken the truth.'

Next, he said, 'Tell me what Spiritual Excellence is.'

The Messenger of Allah, peace and blessings upon him, replied: *'It is to worship Allah as if you see Him, and though you cannot, to know that He sees you.'*

Then, as suddenly as he'd arrived, the stranger left. After a period of silent stupor, Muhammad, peace and blessings upon him, said to Umar, one of his companions who later reported the story, *'Do you know who that questioner was?'*

Umar, may Allah be pleased with him, replied, 'Allah and His Messenger know best.'

The Prophet Muhammad, peace and blessings upon him, said: *'That was Gabriel [the archangel], who came to you [in the form of a man] to teach you your religion.'*

The three dimensions of Islam

There are so many lessons contained within this story, which is called the *hadith* of Gabriel. The dialogue has been preserved for more than 1,400 years, by generations of learned Muslim scholars passing it on to their students. It's contained in the authentic collection of Prophetic sayings.

'Islam' is the name given to the comprehensive religion taught to us by the Prophet Muhammad, peace and blessings upon him. Like all religions, it has three dimensions, which together form the complete faith of Islam:

- **The outward dimension of practices**, which the archangel Gabriel called '*Islam*'
- **The inner dimension of beliefs**, which the archangel called 'Faith,' or '*Iman*'
- **The hidden, spiritual dimension**, which the archangel called 'Spiritual Excellence,' or '*Ihsan*'

All religions differ in their outward practices, and differ somewhat in their belief systems, but they're very similar and point in much the same direction when it comes to the spiritual dimension. In fact, the entire religion of Islam is built on this framework. There are three key areas of study within Islam: law (to do with practices, or *Islam*), creed (to do with beliefs, or *Iman*), and spirituality (to do with the inner dimension, or *Ihsan*).

The leader of Tibetan Buddhism, the Dalai Lama (may Allah preserve, bless and guide him), teaches us that the many religions and spiritual traditions around the world are all wonderful. Each tradition is like a special blend of tea, with particular herbs and leaves that give it a unique and delicious taste. It's not necessary for everyone to have one particular kind of tea, but everyone certainly needs the water in any of the teas to hydrate themselves. The herbs and leaves alone will not save the one dying of thirst.

Unfortunately, there are many people in the modern world who have all the external trappings of material success but avoid the 'tea' of religion due to having tasted some bitter herbs. Even though, like all of us, they desperately need the water.

This 'water' is what Muslims would call the spiritual dimension of religion, or *Ihsan*, and it has two main aspects. The first is inward spiritual evolution and purification. The second is the natural result of this – a more refined and beautiful character. Muslims believe that showing us this path of Spiritual Purification is one of the main reasons Allah (the Infinite Intelligence Behind Life) sent us prophets and messengers throughout the ages, peace and blessings upon them all.[1]

By focusing on the inner, spiritual dimension of Islam, we find ourselves dealing with those aspects of the religion that are completely universal and relevant to everyone. There are certain traits that we all wish to inculcate in ourselves, and which we love to see in other people. For example, love, kindness, patience, compassion, presence, gratitude, and forgiveness are values we tend to appreciate in others and hope to inculcate in ourselves.

Similarly, there are traits that we wish to be free from and don't like to see in other people. Arrogance, hatred, anger, and envy are examples of these, and in Islam, they're known as the 'spiritual diseases' of the heart.

If the religion of Islam were a person, its 'body' would be the outward practices, its 'mind' would be the belief system, and its 'soul' would be the spiritual dimension. But, before I share with you some of the deliciously hydrating tea of Islam, I need to fill you in on a couple of things – like who I am, and how I eventually came to believe in religion.

CHAPTER 2

How I Discovered the Soul of Islam

'Your heart is the size of an ocean.
Go find yourself in its hidden depths.'
RUMI

I was born into a Muslim Pakistani family – the youngest of four children – living in a big house on a windy road in South Manchester in the north of England.

The Maulvi Saab

At the age of eight, I became very excited when my parents suggested I take classes with a 'Maulvi Saab,' the Urdu term for a Quran teacher. This seemed like a wonderful idea because these were to be held in the home of a friend of the family with whose son I went to school. However, it took only one class for me to realize that this was definitely not something I'd enjoy.

My classmates and I were forced to sit in silence for hours. One by one, each of us went to sit with an old, strict Asian man with whom we'd recite the Quran in the middle of the living room. The Quran is written in Arabic, but instead of learning that language, we simply learnt how to pronounce each letter of each word, and then read the book in Arabic without knowing what we were saying. If we mispronounced the letters, or misbehaved, the teacher would grab us by the ear and twist it in a way that made us not want to return to a Quran class ever again.

The most noticeable things about the Maulvi Saab were his grey beard, funny-looking hat, and traditional shalwar kameez outfit – and the unforgettable, very loud way he slurped his tea. He was treated with the utmost respect by our parents, but our mission in life was to get out of those Saturday-morning classes. Each week we'd try hiding behind the curtains and sofas in our respective living rooms, but that didn't work.

Like a donkey carrying books

Over the next couple of years I'd complain more and more to my mother about the classes. I told her that when I was at school, I learnt French so I could read and understand what the books said, but with the Maulvi Saab, I was reciting a book that's supposed to be so important, but I wasn't being taught what it said. 'Doesn't this make us like a donkey carrying very important books on its back?' I asked.

Being a wise woman, my mother, may Allah bless her, agreed with me, but she still made me go to the classes. The simple logic of her cheeky youngest child did have an impact on her though. So much so that for the first time in her life, she started learning Arabic and took a three-year, 650-hour course of detailed Quran study in order to deepen her personal connection with Allah.

My father, may Allah bless him, also made us go to these classes, but he put a huge emphasis on formal study. Growing up in a village in Pakistan, he'd had to cycle 16km (10 miles) to get to the local school, and over the next couple of decades, through hard work and grit, he somehow made his way to England as a professional chartered accountant.

Now that his own children had it so easy, and were put through the best schools, he wasn't going to take it easy on us. He didn't care much for the Maulvi Saab, but if our regular schoolteacher had anything less than extremely positive things to say about us, we were in real trouble. To give you a frame of reference, when I was 16, I received 10 'A' grades in my exams, but was very frightened to break the news to my dad because I didn't get any A-star grades.

Like many Muslims of my generation, I found that Islam had been reduced to dry, ritualistic practices without real meaning; we had no idea how doing these things was supposed to improve our lives. Reciting a book you don't understand, praying with memorized words you don't know the meaning of, and for one month every year, spending hours each day without eating or drinking. To me, this seemed like a very arduous and somewhat inconvenient religion. But I never dared speak about it in that way – at least, not in front of the adults.

Are you really a Muslim?

When I was 11, the family took a summer holiday in Pakistan. We did this annually, but that particular year was extra special. My father had decided that we would spend a few weeks in Pakistan, and then a couple of weeks in the Holy Cities of Mecca and Medina in Saudi Arabia, to do the *Umra*, an optional pilgrimage to Mecca.

Because of this, the topic of religion was brought up more often than usual, especially by my uncle – the husband of my mother's sister. My aunt was the softest, gentlest of women, and would always make us laugh. She ran a very inexpensive school for poor children in Islamabad, Pakistan's capital, and would sometimes ask me to look at the pupils' English homework, which made me feel very intelligent.

Her husband, on the other hand, seemed to us kids to be the strictest, harshest of men – we were all afraid to laugh, or act smart, in front of him. One evening, for some logistical reason, my brother and I were stuck with my uncle. A highly intimidating powerhouse of a man with a deliberately, perfectly trimmed moustache, he'd hold his cigar in a way that let you know he'd earned the right to it.

He was a retired colonel in Pakistan's army and had a very large collection of guns in his home, but that wasn't the intimidating part. It was the intense way he'd look at you, as if he could see through your skin and bones and directly into your soul. A bullet could whizz past his head, and he wouldn't even flinch, let alone drop his cigar.

On this particular evening, which was largely made up of long, awkward silences, my uncle challenged me and my brother. As he quoted thought-provoking excerpts from the book he was reading, *The Road To Mecca* by Muhammad Asad, he asked us questions about them. It was the first time I'd ever really stopped to think about religion in a serious way. At one point my uncle looked at us intently and in perfect English, with the accent of a highly educated Pakistani man, he said:

'You have to decide for yourself if you really believe that Allah exists. And if you say that He does, you have to decide for yourself whether the Quran is the Word of God or not. If you say it is, then you must accept all of it, and if you say it's not, you must reject all of it.

'Because it all came from the same source. Either the Prophet, peace and blessings upon him, was truthful, or he was insane, or he was a liar. Wherever you stand, be sure, and stand there firmly. There's nothing worse than hypocrisy.'

It was an intense experience, but there was something so simple and true about what my uncle was saying. Over the years, I've come to really appreciate that advice. He didn't tell us the answers, but he at least got us asking the right questions. From then on, I knew I would either be a true believer or a true atheist, but nothing in between.

My first truly spiritual experience

Before I knew it, my family and I had reached the end of our own long journey to Mecca, wearing the full traditional garb of just two simple sheets. We had traveled through the night, and as soon as we arrived at the hotel I lay down on the bed, only to be told off by my mother: 'Don't lie down, we're going to the Holy Mosque!' I was so tired, I thought she was joking.

A few minutes later, we arrived at a huge mosque, the likes of which I'd never seen. I was used to praying in a cramped basement near a shopping mall in cold, grey Manchester, but this was a spacious marble palace. There was an excitement and spiritual energy to being there that overcame me. We kept walking toward the center of the Holy Mosque. Dressed in the most humble clothes, we were in a place fit for royalty. And that's when I saw her.

Have you ever seen images on TV of the Kaba in Mecca – the most sacred site in Islam? She looks like a black cube, and is usually pictured with tens of thousands of people walking around her. The images are nothing compared to being there in person. When I first laid eyes on her, my mind went completely blank. I had no words or labels to describe this sight, and no way of explaining the joyful sense of peace that overtook me.

The space between seeing something and being able to label or describe it, is perhaps the purest form of 'beauty.' Many years later, I realized that this had been a transcendent, spiritual experience. From that point on, it was impossible for me not to believe in Allah. I'd somehow witnessed the divine presence, but not with my eyes.

Putting God on trial

Despite my newfound faith, I didn't yet have the logic to back it up. When I returned to school after our trip to Mecca, my very intelligent classmates helped me develop this logic – because most of them were atheists. A couple of years into high school, I'd discover that most of my friends thought that the idea of God was laughable.

Real discussion about the existence of God and the meaning of life only took place in Religious Education classes. In those, we explored the major world religions on a very basic level, but the best part was debating the question, 'Does God exist?' and doing an exercise in which we 'put God on trial.' We set up a jury and like lawyers, put forward all the major arguments for and against the existence of God. And then we took a vote. The class unanimously decided that the answer to the question was: 'No, of course not.'

This is one of the travesties of the postmodern education system: the underlying assumption that if you're really intelligent, and don't buy into the myths that the masses believe in, the logical conclusion you'll come to is that God does not exist. Atheism, an *unprovable* belief system, is taken as the gospel truth.

I didn't buy it. I got full marks in the Religion and Philosophy class. And I knew that I now held a belief that my classmates did not. A belief that they couldn't disprove. The belief that Allah exists and the Quran is divine revelation.

The problem with faith in schools

When it came to religion, the biggest problem facing my generation of Muslims was that the Maulvi Saab characters had no idea what life was like for those of us growing up in the West. Nor were they able to respond to our most basic, existential questions, most of which they'd never had to answer before.

My Urdu was at a basic conversational level, and was definitely not good enough to have a deeply philosophical conversation. Even if the Maulvi Saabs had had the answers to these questions, there was so little connection between me and them, I wouldn't have been inclined to find out.

What I wanted to know was this: why do we pray that way? Is there any point to Ramadan? Is all of this supposed to improve your life somehow, or are these just boxes you need to tick to go to Heaven? And most importantly: is it true that non-Muslims go to Hell, and Muslims don't, even though they're good people who are just like us? This last question was kind of a deal-breaker for me. There was no logical reason I could see why my friends at school didn't deserve the same fair chance at Paradise as I did.

I don't think my parents ever had to think about these things at that young age, because they didn't grow up with all of their friends not sharing their religion. And, like the Maulvi Saabs, they didn't realize that the education system we were supposed to ace our way through was training us to look down on religion. We were led to believe that a 'free-thinking,' independent mind would come to the conclusion that God doesn't really exist and that religion is, as Karl Max said, just the 'opium of the people.'

It struck me that this was a bizarre belief for virtually *everyone* in my class to have come to in unison. If religion was the opium of the people, why was it that the believers in religion were a tiny minority in the class? How had these free-thinking students come to exactly the same conclusions as their parents and teachers? They had clearly ingested a different, but equally effective, opiate.

> 'When it is said to them, "Follow the message that God has sent down," they answer,
> "We follow the ways of our forefathers." Really? Even though their forefathers understood nothing and were not guided?'[1]
>
> QURAN

For the most part, these conversations about the existence of God, and the beliefs that may result from this question, were interesting, but they didn't matter too much to me at that stage. During break times at school, these issues were nowhere near as important to me as Manchester United football club, Bruce Lee, and the latest episode of *The X-Files*.

My first real Islam teacher

By the age of 15, I believed in the existence of Allah, and thought that Islam was probably a decent enough religion, with a supposedly amazing book of revelation that was, unfortunately, pretty much unreadable in English. So I would attend Friday prayer at school, which was organized by the older boys.

And then I met him: the knowledgeable, cool guy who inspired me to take things to the next level. May Allah increase him in light, and continue to bless him and reward him for his devotion to the path of Islam. His name, would you believe it, was Muhammad.

He was doing a degree in philosophy at the University of Manchester and was running their Islamic Society, so I figured he must know his stuff. Legend had it that he'd spent a whole month studying with an American scholar called Shaykh Hamza Yusuf. And he'd read Aristotle.

Finally, I'd met my match: someone who was as religious as the Maulvi Saab, but cooler than me. I asked him *everything*:

'Why do you believe in God, and can you prove He really exists?' 'What do you say about evolution?' 'Is it true that you're supposed to chop people's hands off if they steal (and isn't that a bit harsh)?'

'Is right right and wrong wrong, or did God create right and wrong?' 'If there really is a God, why is there so much suffering in the world?' 'Are we allowed to have girlfriends?' 'Oh, and given that God is all-Merciful and all-Just, do all non-Muslims go to Hell?' And Muhammad had the answers. (When he answered that last question sensibly, I knew I could trust him with the others.)

The older boys arranged for Muhammad to come in to our school on Wednesday lunchtimes and hold a talk in which he *really* went into things. No matter how much time I got with him, I always wanted more, and Wednesday lunchtime became the highlight of my week. I wanted to be like Muhammad when I finished school, and I soon made the commitment to pray five times a day. I also started listening to audio recordings of Shaykh Hamza Yusuf.

A couple of years later, I went to a 'study circle' in Muhammad's dorm room on a Wednesday evening. It was an advanced class, and the other attendees were university students. On one occasion, I spent the night at his home and when we awoke early the next morning, we got ready and walked to the nearby student mosque for the pre-dawn *Fajr* prayer (the first of the five daily prayers in Islam). On the way over, Muhammad recited a chapter of the Quran from memory, and when I left for school that morning, I was a new man.

That was the first time I'd prayed *Fajr* in a mosque, aside from my time in Mecca all those years previously. On this occasion it was because I wanted to, not because my parents made me. I was filled with the same spiritual energy I'd touched on in the Holy Land, but I was still in Manchester. Later that day, the minute I entered the classroom, my friends noticed that I was on a total high. If this was the opium of the people, I wanted more.

Where were you on 9/11?

By the last year of high school, I was a surprisingly devout Muslim. I only did the things that made sense to me, but then it *all* made sense to me. I prayed five times a day, which made me the default head of our school's Islamic Society.

I loved having conversations about religion and philosophy, and it became clearer and clearer to me that the only reason my classmates didn't believe in Islam, was that they didn't have access to the teachers, books, logic, and wisdom that I'd been blessed with. It seemed that I'd inherited a treasure from my parents that most of my classmates didn't have such easy access to.

And then, on a typical Tuesday afternoon, in the middle of an uninteresting statistics class, it happened. 'They're saying Palestinians hijacked a plane and did this intentionally,' said the teacher, who'd set us exercises to work on so he could pop back and forth to the staff room to watch the events unfold live on TV. Next update: 'The Palestinian authorities are denying any responsibility, but the hijackers are definitely Muslims.' The students looked at me. I just shrugged and shook my head.

By 3:45 p.m. both towers of the World Trade Center had fallen, and I was on my way to a local nursing home with my friend Matthew to spend time with the elderly. In order to get into medical school, which was my aim at the time, you have to prove that you actually care about people, so our school helped us find volunteering gigs with the local community.

On the walk over, there could only be one topic of conversation. Matthew: 'This is massive. This is so huge. This is going to change politics and everything. I bet, like 20 years from now, we'll still be talking about this and we'll still remember where we were when it happened.' He was a smart guy.

Matthew's mother, may Allah bless her, picked us up an hour later and we listened to the news on the way home. 'Hmm… that's weird,' I said. 'They just called it *Islamic* terrorism. That doesn't make sense. How can mass murder possibly be "Islamic?"' Matthew and his mother agreed with me.

Although at the time I thought that the events of that day would affect world politics, I had absolutely no idea of the impact they would have on me and my community over the next few years.

Study medicine, or save the world?

All that community volunteering must have worked, because a year later, I was at medical school at the University of Manchester. I spent the long summer holiday between school and university taking Arabic and Islamic studies courses. I was passionate about learning more, and I discovered that there's a serious rigor to Islamic scholarship.

One of our teachers remarked that he'd been studying, on average, six days a week for eight hours a day, and felt as if he hadn't gained more than a drop within an ocean of knowledge. After studying for the whole summer, I figured that I now perhaps had a drop of his drop. And I was very thirsty.

Within the first half-term of my medical studies, despite already having established a great set of friends and a social network thanks to the university's Islamic Society, I became disillusioned with my degree. I'd always wanted to be a doctor… Or so I believed. The truth was that I hadn't really given it much thought. It's just that, if you're an Asian lad and you're smart enough to get into medical school, you do it. Leaving isn't an option. But then, I was never great at sticking to the rules.

I spent far more time immersed in this new world of Islam than I did studying medicine. There were lectures, conferences, and study circles, and my housemate was one of the guys who'd joined the Wednesday evening gatherings at Muhammad's a couple of years earlier. He'd converted to Islam and could now recite the Quran beautifully; he'd memorized much of it, and had a way of logically and beautifully interpreting it. And, notably, he was a core organizer of the Stop The War movement on campus.

In my first year at university, I watched as 2 million people, including almost all the Muslims I knew, took to the streets of London to plead with the government not to take the UK to war with Iraq. Shortly afterward, we were at war with Iraq. This was a country that had absolutely nothing to do with 9/11, but it did have plenty of oil and a cocky leader. So, over the next decade, the UK and its allies inflicted, in terms of loss of life, the equivalent of 50 consecutive 9/11s on Iraq's civilian population (and that's a conservative estimate).

It occurred to me that there are two types of people in the world: those who care about all human life equally, and those who care about people 'like us,' more than people 'like them.' Some Muslims cared more about the Iraqis than the Americans. Some Brits, including most politicians, definitely cared more about Brits and Americans than Iraqis or Afghanis. To me, and to most people who weren't touting a political agenda, it didn't matter who the victim was, or who the attacker was. As the Quran puts it: to kill one innocent life is like killing all of humanity.

I didn't really have any interest in politics before I went to university. I just wanted more of that sweet honey of spiritual bliss that I was gifted little tastes of in Mecca, and later in that pre-dawn *Fajr* prayer. But before I could dive into an ocean of spirituality, I had to face the fact that being a practicing Muslim meant confronting politics.

On our campus at that time, the lefties were all over the Muslims because they knew we were allies in the fight against an unjust war. Those on the right were all over them too, because if you opposed the war in Iraq, it was as if you were supporting terrorism – especially if you were a brown Muslim. I remember waiting in line at a Chinese take-out restaurant near the campus and overhearing a girl say on her phone, 'Wait, but why would you be *against* the War on Terror? Surely terror is a bad thing?!'

In the midst of all this, one thing became crystal clear to me: I definitely had to do something about the state of the world, and becoming a doctor – as noble as that profession is – just didn't fit in with my plans to 'change the world.'

My love affair

It was on a depressing Friday night at my parents' house that my love affair with personal growth began. Although I was in my early 20s by then, and living on campus, my dad would insist that at 5 p.m. every Friday, regardless of what I had going on at university, I get in the car and go home with him. And because I was very afraid of him, I obliged. It was a method of keeping me under control and out of trouble. The problem was, I was already in trouble – I just didn't know how to break the news to him.

I was watching television as usual, when I came across one of those infomercials. It was set on a beach in California and featured a big American guy called Tony Robbins talking about how terrible his life had been, but then he discovered the secrets of psychology, and now his life was awesome. And in this new seven-day program he'd share all the secrets of having the body, relationships, time-management skills, and mindset we all need in order to thrive – at the special low price of just $99 or three easy payments of $39.99.

As embarrassing as it is for the conservative, reserved Brit inside me to admit, I was a total sucker for this 30-minute advert. I must have watched it at least a dozen times over the next few days. I don't know what it was about it...

Perhaps it was that I'd fallen in love with a white, Spanish, non-Muslim girl at university. Perhaps it was that I'd decided I wanted to quit medical school. Perhaps it was that, deep down inside, I knew that I wanted to travel the world, maybe live in a desert, and definitely learn Arabic and find a spiritual master, the way Shaykh Hamza Yusuf did. Perhaps it was that I could really see myself on a beach in California some day.

Whatever the reason, I do know that I had absolutely no way of knowing how to explain any of these dreams to my dad. And maybe Tony Robbins could help.

Enter the 'Quran Coach'

Three years later I was in Egypt: halfway through a degree in Arabic, a skilled practitioner of Neuro-Linguistic Programming (NLP), and married to a woman who lived in Spain, even though I had no income beyond a very tight student loan. But I was doing it: I was living the dream. I now had the ability to read the Quran in Arabic, and actually understand it. And I had the ability to coach people and help them make big changes in their lives, too.

At some point it occurred to me that if I put two and two together, I could probably coach other young Muslims who wanted to understand their faith more deeply by learning Arabic – and I was sure I could help them do it in much less time than it had taken me. I realized that you don't need a degree in Arabic, and you don't need to spend years living in a Muslim country.

To reach the point where you can understand the Quran directly in Arabic, without needing an English translation, only takes about twelve weeks, provided you're willing to study for about half an hour a day, take a weekly class, and find a good teacher. Pretty soon I had my own blog, and became known as the 'Quran Coach.' That blog – Quran For Busy People – still benefits readers to this day and has many articles, audios, and videos designed to help Western Muslims deepen their connection to the divine.

Sometimes clients would ask me why I chose to become a coach instead of just studying more and becoming a scholar.

The truth is, I felt like I could be of more benefit to humanity as a friend – or coach – who could empower people and help them succeed, rather than as a scholar who would tell them what to do. As the Prophet Muhammad, peace and blessings upon him, said:

> *'The best of people are those that bring the most benefit to the rest of mankind.'*[2]

I guess I was inspired to become a coach because, when it really came down to it, it wasn't the scholars and preachers who'd helped me fulfill my dreams, face my fears, and ultimately come closer to Allah. Rather, it was the authors of the dozens of personal development books and courses I'd studied, and my coaches at the time, may Allah bless them all for their sincere efforts to benefit humanity.

The truth is that at this point in my life, I still hadn't really discovered the 'soul' of Islam, just parts of its 'body' and 'mind' that I was struggling to study and implement. Perhaps that's why, even as I was helping my brothers and sisters to come closer to the Quran, something else was going on inside me.

Burning myself out

> 'Do you enjoin people to do good, and forget it yourself, even though you recite the Book? Have you no sense?'[3]
>
> QURAN

'A person who teaches goodness to others, while neglecting his own soul, is like an oil lamp that illumines others while burning itself out.'[4]

The Prophet Muhammad, peace and blessings upon him

This Quran verse and Prophetic teaching summed me up in a nutshell. I could tell there was something 'off' about my approach, despite the fact that people were loving it. There were two problems that were playing at the back of my mind, preoccupying me and causing burnout.

The first was that it seemed bizarre that I was using NLP and a host of other personal development 'techniques' to help people study the Quran, when the Quran itself is supposed to be the greatest personal development manual of all time. I wasn't going into the Quran to see how it could transform our lives.

I was depending on 'Western' techniques with no basis in Islam that I could see, and using them to help people study. There's nothing intrinsically wrong with this – anything of truth that's beneficial is intrinsically 'Islamic' – I just had a niggling sensation that I must have been missing something.

The second problem was that, even though over the years I'd come to master many coaching and personal development techniques, I had a big problem in my own personal life. I'd seen counselors, coaches, and therapists to help resolve it, but I remained stuck. My marriage was falling apart. Despite all the personal growth training, and all the traditional studying of Islam, when it really came down to it, my wife and I were both unhappy.

Crisis of faith

The issue of my failing marriage left me skeptical, and eventually even a little cynical, of personal growth, and even of Islam. I thought to myself: *I'm a decent enough guy and I'm devoted to learning more and trying to do better, but none of the advice out there on how to improve relationships is working for me.*

I'd studied the '*fiqh*' (Islamic laws) of marriage, and that didn't help. And at some point I realized that it wasn't supposed to. The Islamic laws of marriage improve your relationship about as much as the Islamic laws of slaughter improve your cooking. I was looking to the 'body' of Islam to improve the 'soul' of my marriage, but it doesn't work that way.

Soon, friends from England who visited me in Barcelona, where I lived with my then wife, would gently nudge me in the direction of introspection. It was obvious something wasn't working. I was becoming weaker, spiritually and emotionally, which didn't bode well for my role as a 'life coach.' My wife and I were soon divorced, and immediately after the sudden shock of the end of my first love relationship, I was ready for a change.

To recover from the pain of the breakup, I spoke with an Indian guru, attended a relationship workshop in Las Vegas, and spoke with yet another coach. *Maybe the next one will have the answers*, I thought. The Muslims I knew at the time didn't seem to have them – and I couldn't bear the self-righteousness of the community, or the 'serves you right for going for a non-Muslim girl' attitude.

I watched relationship-training videos about getting over a breakup; they didn't help. I embarked on a fitness rampage and arranged with an old school friend to spend a month just focused on eating and training, as if we were in the military. We got our bodies in great shape, but the underlying problem, and my unspoken depression, remained.

It seemed that this time, there was no quick fix and no shortcuts. I started to wonder whether I'd completely lost the plot. Both the personal growth industry and the Islamic path had forsaken me. I was alone, and although my body was strong, my heart was broken.

The key that unlocked the treasure

'If the heart does not break open, how will the Light enter?'

Rumi

There are great transformational teachings inside of Islam and, as far as I can tell, all true spiritual traditions. Scholars of Islam would always say this, but Allah, the Most Loving, hadn't yet lifted the veils that were blocking me from seeing it. I was reading the Quran in Arabic, but I still couldn't understand the depth of it. The light of spiritual truth was already within me, but I was looking all around me, unable to find it. I was willing to travel anywhere to get out of pain, but I wasn't journeying to the one place where the solution lay: within.

On one ordinary weekday in the apartment I was renting in Barcelona, I woke up late, feeling depressed, and beating myself up because I'd missed the pre-dawn *Fajr* prayer, yet again. What I didn't realize on that sunny morning was that later that day, my life would change forever.

I received a phone call from one of the coaches I'd contacted earlier in the week. During the conversation, I explained to this essentially random stranger that I'd been through a really tough breakup about nine months earlier and didn't really know how to handle it. She had been my first love, I told him; I was depressed, I felt guilty, angry, and I was lonely.

The coach, may Allah guide, bless, and reward him, listened deeply, with total presence. I hadn't opened up about this stuff to anyone in the way I laid it all out to him. I can now see how that conversation impacted me, permanently.

He asked me: 'You know that your feelings of loneliness, depression, and guilt aren't coming from the divorce, right? They're coming from your thinking.' After many years in the personal growth field I'd come to understand that my thinking had something to do with my feelings. So when I first heard the coach say this, I ignorantly replied, 'Oh, yeah, well I know that.'

Looking back, I can imagine him smiling as I said that. It was the classic arrogant response of someone who's about to undergo a transformation that will lead to lifelong humility. His next statement changed my world.

'No, no, no... It's not that some of your feelings come in part from your thinking. I mean *100 percent* of everything you're feeling right now: *100 percent* of that loneliness, sadness, anger and guilt... All of it is coming from your thought. Literally zero percent of it is coming from your old relationship or the breakup. None of your feelings is coming from that.'

My mind went completely quiet and I felt a shudder through my entire body. It was a warm, comfortable shudder that came with a kind of deep knowing that nothing would be the same again. In that moment, I had a realization that came from deep within. It was as though all of my limiting beliefs and 'issues' disappeared in about four seconds. The experience was nothing short of spiritual. It was a feeling I would come to enjoy many times again, albeit much more subtly. The floodgates were now open.

Everything I'd been studying in personal growth and Islam had suddenly fallen into place in a way that was relevant and accessible to me. I couldn't see this at the time, though. Then, I was just quiet. In fact, my mind was quieter than it had been in years. I was later told that I fell completely silent for the better part of 10 or 15 minutes.

This is the most important thing to understand about the spiritual truth I'd just discovered: it makes perfect common sense. Intellectually, it doesn't do all that much for you. And yet, when you see the multitude of ways in which we're living our lives as though this spiritual law isn't true, everything changes.

I didn't know it then, but with this one insight, the depth and wisdom of the Quran was suddenly open to me. The 'Soul of Islam' had become as clear and visible to me as the laptop on which I'm typing these words. I'm guessing that none of this makes much sense to you yet. So, perhaps it's time I share with you the psychological, spiritual understanding that transformed my life.

CHAPTER 3

Uncovering Spiritual Reality

'Thought is the missing link that gives us the power to recognize the illusory separation between the spiritual world and the world of form.'[1]

SYDNEY BANKS

After that insightful moment several years ago, I immediately sought out the source of the understanding that my new coach was pointing me toward. I soon found myself learning from Keith Blevens, PhD, and his wife, Valda Monroe, co-founders of the 'Inside-Out Paradigm' (also known as the 'Three Principles Paradigm.')

Teaching the Inside-Out Paradigm has become my life's work, to the point that it's virtually impossible for me to talk in any depth about the spiritual dimension of Islam without it. With this understanding, the Quran and the Prophetic teachings have become a continuous source of insight and healing for me, and everyone I work with.

The Inside-Out Paradigm isn't based on any psychological 'theory' or philosophy. Neither is it cultural, moral, or religious – it's based on neutral, psychological, unchanging *principles*. As such, it's of benefit to everyone, irrespective of background. These principles marry us all to the spiritual, whether or not we're conscious of it. They are the psychology of Islam, because they are the psychology of everyone.

The enlightened welder

'Seek knowledge, even to China.'[2]

THE PROPHET, PEACE AND BLESSINGS UPON HIM

Keith Blevens and Valda Monroe are long-time students of a man named Sydney Banks, may he rest in peace. Banks was a manual laborer with a ninth-grade education who had read three books in his life – all of them about welding. However, in 1973, when he was 43 years old, he had a sudden flash of insight.

In what he described as an 'enlightening experience,' he instantly knew 'the true meaning of God.' He turned and said to his stunned wife and mother-in-law: 'What I just learnt will change psychology and psychiatry.' He had insightfully uncovered what he later termed the 'Three Principles' of Mind, Consciousness, and Thought.[3]

Banks spent the rest of his life sharing what he'd uncovered. He entrusted his final works to Keith and Valda, who've spent nearly four decades rigorously studying his recordings, writings, and teachings. It's their contention, and mine, that these Three Principles form the paradigm that the field of psychology has long been searching for.

A true paradigm

A paradigm is a worldview underlying the methodology of a particular scientific subject: in this case, psychology. A true paradigm of psychology would have to be universal and constant. It wouldn't have exceptions or anomalies, and it couldn't change according to time, place, personality, or situation. It would need to explain *all* human psychological functioning.

William James, the father of modern American psychology who wrote *The Principles of Psychology* in 1890, humbly acknowledged that no such law or constant had yet been uncovered. 'We do not even know the terms with which these elementary laws would obtain, if we had them,' he said. 'This is no science, this is only the hope of a science.' In the absence of a paradigm governing a subject, there's a proliferation of theories, myths, and assumptions about how that area works.[4]

Throughout history, it's always been enlightening when humans have been able to distinguish the way something actually works from how it doesn't work. There are few examples of these true 'paradigm shifts' that have changed the way we think about scientific subjects.

Newton's Laws of Motion and Universal Gravitation changed the way we approach and think about physics. For millennia, we believed that the Earth was the center of the Universe. Then came the Copernican revolution in the sixteenth century, which changed the way we view the solar system and our place in it. Semmelweis's Germ Theory changed the way we think about medicine, and affected our everyday approach to hygiene.

Psychology, as a field, has been without a true paradigm. William James said that when such laws or constants *were* uncovered, they would make the importance of all the discoveries humanity has made technologically since fire pale in comparison.[5]

Introducing the 'Inside-Out' Paradigm

The Inside-Out Paradigm states that the Three Principles of Mind, Consciousness, and Thought constitute the true paradigm of psychology. This is a *constant paradigm* based on three fundamental principles that are ever present and unchanging – without exception – and therefore predictable. It states that all experience comes to us only in one way: through the irreducible elements of Mind, Consciousness, and Thought.

The Inside-Out Paradigm doesn't tell people what to think or what to feel. It's descriptive, not prescriptive. It provides a profound explanation for human psychological and spiritual experience that's a deeper understanding than anything we've previously known.

Through the Inside-Out Paradigm, we discover a deeper foundation and organization to human experience that *changes the questions we ask*. Rather than asking, 'How do I make myself feel better?' or 'How can I improve myself?', the deeper question now becomes: 'How does our experience of life actually work, psychologically and spiritually?' Many other questions of human psychology are resolved or rendered obsolete by answering this accurately.

The insight of the Inside-Out Paradigm can be most simply expressed as:

Feelings are coming from thought in the moment.

Other ways of putting this across are:

- All feelings, attitudes, states of mind, realities, and experiences are coming from our use of the Universal Principles of Mind, Consciousness, and Thought, in the moment.
- Feelings are always coming from the Universal Principle of Thought in the moment.
- Or, as Keith Blevens once put it: 'We are living in the feeling of our thinking, moment to moment.'[6]

The point is that there's just one specific way through which all of humanity experiences feeling, which is this:

We will only ever feel our thought in the moment.

As soon as our thought – or our *way of thinking* – changes, our feelings change, even if the situation or object we're thinking about stays the same. Feeling and thought are inseparable; they are two sides of the same coin. Nothing other than thought in a given moment can cause feeling in that same moment. We may not be aware of our thinking, or be able to change it instantly, but we're always feeling our thinking, whether it's conscious or unconscious.

Knowing that there's only one way, one truth, through which all experience occurs, is what makes this the true psychology. It gives us a tremendous black-and-white criteria we can use to distinguish reality from illusion. It's not a 'good/bad,' or 'right/wrong,' or 'positive/negative,' or 'high mood/low mood' criteria. It's a 'how our psychological/spiritual system actually works' versus 'how our psychological/spiritual system actually doesn't work' criteria.

As such, it's surprisingly helpful to us. It becomes less and less tempting to spend time ruminating on something that you *know* is impossible. I've never worried about falling off the face of the Earth – because I know that the Earth is spherical. In the same way, it's becoming increasingly difficult for me to worry about how a situation or person or circumstance will make me feel, because I now know that feelings can only come from thought in the moment, and never from any situation.

The Inside-Out is a universal law, and although you may have previously heard of the thought-feeling connection, this is likely the first time you've ever thought of it as an absolute. It's a universal, principle-based, pre-existing, unbreakable *law* of human psychology.

All reality is spiritual

> *'We are not human beings having a spiritual experience. We are spiritual beings having a human experience.'*
>
> **Pierre Teilhard de Chardin**

Thought is not a 'thing.' It's a neutral, formless, 'spiritual' energy. The fact that all of our experience is manifested through 'thought,' 'consciousness,' and 'mind,' means that we are all 'spiritual beings having a human experience.' This is no longer a matter of belief. There is simply no way of having any experience without these formless 'spiritual/ psychological' principles. All experience occurs from the 'Inside-Out,' which is to say, from these three psychological elements.

Within this Inside-Out understanding lies the cure for all psychological and spiritual diseases. As Sydney Banks put it:

'The sicknesses of the mind are feelings that we create and put onto objects. But if you can see the objects without the feelings, you are healthy.'[7]

Awareness that feeling comes from thought in the moment defines mental health. The illusion that feeling comes from somewhere other than thought in the moment, can be pinpointed as the precise starting point of mental illness and psychological suffering.

In the words of Valda Monroe: 'When we split feeling from thought, we create an illusory outside. We create ego. This is precisely where all human problems begin, and end. All human problems are paradigm problems. This is the logic and wisdom of the Three Principles (Inside-Out) Paradigm.'

Effortless transformation

Do you realize what we're saying here? All anger, frustration, sadness, envy, hurt, and guilt come from the way we're thinking in the moment and not from the situation, person, or problem we're thinking about. On the other hand, all happiness, joy, bliss, love, peace, and excitement also come from the way we're thinking in the moment, and not the situation, person, or circumstance we're thinking about.

This reality explains all human psychological functioning. I'm not saying that you 'should believe' that feeling comes from thought. I'm saying that this is *absolutely true*, no matter what you believe. Recognizing this as a fact is transformative for any individual. Part II of this book is designed to help you experience this transformation, through a series of personal stories and anecdotes. Each of the chapters covers a theme, such as 'Loving Kindness,' 'Peace,' and 'Presence,' all of which become lived realities from the Inside-Out.

Transcending the Outside-In Illusion

'The problem is not your thinking. The problem is believing that your feelings are coming from something other than thought in the moment. Feelings/Experience/ Reality is being created always, only, this one way.'

Valda Monroe

Here's the key: our problem has never been that feelings come from thought in the moment – that's just a psychological fact. Our only problem has been *the false belief that something other than thought in the moment* can cause our feelings. That belief is, by definition, the 'Outside-In Illusion.' When we become aware of this trap, we're less inclined to fall into it, and we can catch ourselves when we do. The best part is, every single time we see through this illusion, we transform.

It's easy to think that the situations and circumstances of our lives, or the past we've lived through, are the cause of our current-moment feelings. However, this is never the case.

The moment we switch from believing that the 'outside' is causing our feelings, in any given context, to insightfully realizing that actually, our own thought is causing our feelings in this moment, is the moment we drop ego. This insightful realization changes us in unpredictably positive ways.

I could give you 100 stories of permanent changes that have occurred in my own life, and each of my clients could give you 100 stories of changes in their life – and they would all point to this truth as the source of that transformation. Part II of this book shares some of these stories, and shows how people have started living into the universal values of Islam through this psychological understanding.

The moment it becomes clear to us that our psychological system is set up in such a way that *nothing* other than thought in the moment has the power to cause a feeling, is the moment we start moving in the direction of unavoidable spiritual evolution. It's like getting on a train that moves us toward deeper, more insightful knowledge.

The source of spiritual evolution

The more deeply we look in this direction, the more we spiritually evolve, understand ourselves, and come to a deeper knowledge of Allah, the Transcendent. This evolution happens through insightful realization, which is a gift from Allah, and not something we can achieve through our own effort. In this sense, it is 'effortless.'

Insightful realization, spiritual growth, and deeper feelings of love and connection with the divine are not readily available to us while we're being fooled by the Outside-In Illusion. But they hit us like a ton of bricks when we're Inside-Out.

After many years of studying and teaching personal development, this is the first time I've ever come across an understanding of psychology that leads to an automatic, effortless embodiment of the virtues taught by Islam, and indeed all religions and spiritual traditions. Acknowledging the truth that feelings are always coming from thought in the moment continues to make me a better person, and a better Muslim, and for this, I'm deeply grateful to Allah, the Source of Insight.

'Insight is what occurs when our ego collapses over a particular subject.'

Sydney Banks

So, what if the 'particular subject' we wanted to look at insightfully was Islam? What if we could get away from the drama, the emotions, and the feelings that we attach to religion, and instead take an objective, deep look into the teachings themselves? What would happen if we were to embark on an exploration of Islam based on insight, not ego? What would it be like to truly live Islam from the Inside-Out?

Living Islam from the Inside-Out

Thought is a divine gift and a spiritual power, given to us by Allah. We can use this power to think anything we want. All feeling comes from the way we use this gift.

As Muslims we say: 'There is no might or power, except Allah.' An impactful way in which I think of this now is: 'There is no might or power to cause our feelings, except Allah, through the divine gift of thought in this moment.'

Knowing that my felt experience of life has always been coming from the way I use this God-given power of thought in the moment, opened a fresh door from which I could explore the depth and beauty of the religion of Islam. I can now look at Islam with the humble realization that for most of my life, I'd innocently been approaching life and religion from the non-existent Outside-In Illusion.

From this place of misunderstanding, the spiritual depth of Islam was closed to me. Spiritual insight occurs when we align with the 'Inside-Out Reality.' This has always been true, for everyone, even before we developed this terminology to talk about such experiences.

To 'live Islam from the Inside-Out' is to take an insightful look at the teachings of the Quran and the Prophet Muhammad, peace and blessings upon him, based on the knowledge that Allah gives us our experience and feelings through the spiritual gift of thought. This is a new paradigm from which to view the world, and the religion. Since I started seeing Islam from this perspective, all I've found is an ever-deepening sense of love, beauty, and spiritual depth. This book is an attempt to share these gifts with you.

The chapters in Part II explore some of the most essential spiritual teachings of the religion of Islam. These teachings are followed by my own personal insights, reflections, and stories of how impossible they can be to try and embody when we operate from the Outside-In Illusion, and how effortless and natural it becomes to live Islam when we see the truth of the Inside-Out Reality.

In other words, by looking at Islam from the Inside-Out, we're all able to look into the 'Soul of Islam.' And we can all be touched, even transformed, by the spiritual wisdom of the 'Soul of Islam,' if Allah wills it.

CHAPTER 4

Quran – the Divine Revelation

'Allah: there is no god but Him, the Ever Living,
the Ever Watchful. Step by step,
He has sent the Scripture down to you [Prophet]
with the Truth, confirming what went before:
He sent down the Torah and the Gospel.'[1]

QURAN

Now that you've been introduced to the 'Soul of Islam,' and to the Inside-Out Paradigm, there's one more element to come before we can embark on this spiritual journey together. We need to explore a whole new world – that of the Quran, the holy book of Islam.

I'll start with how the Quran was revealed and preserved, the three main concepts contained within its message, and who it was revealed for. Then we'll look at the 'infamous' *Shariah*, whose primary source is the Quran, and I'll present some clarifying Quranic frameworks. Along the way, we'll meet some brilliant, inspiring Muslim women who are at the forefront of preserving the Quranic message.

The revelation of the Quran

Muslims believe that the Quran is a divine revelation from God, given to the Prophet Muhammad, peace and blessings upon him, through the Archangel Gabriel, for the benefit of humanity. Quran literally means 'Recitation.'

The word 'Quran' is derived from the Arabic word 'to recite,' or 'to read.' The Quran is not the book we hold in our hands, but the sound that comes from us when we recite it in the precise manner taught to us by the Prophet. It was revealed to him over the course of 23 years, from the ages of 40 to 63.

The Quran is distinct, in both style and substance, from the everyday speech of the Prophet, peace and blessings upon him. Something that the Prophet said, which isn't part of the body of the Quran, is called a '*hadith*.' These 'Prophetic sayings,' along with accounts of the Prophet's daily practice, form the 'Sunnah,' or 'Prophetic example.'

After the Quran, the Sunnah is the second major source of guidance for Muslims. In this book, I refer to these *hadiths* simply as 'Prophetic sayings.' The Quran and Sunnah are the primary scriptural sources of Islam.

The order and transmission of the Quran

The order in which we read the Quran today is not the chronological order in which it was revealed to the Prophet, peace and blessings upon him. Each year during the month of Ramadan (the holiest of the 12 lunar months in the Islamic calendar), the Prophet would review all of the revelation that had been revealed so far with the Archangel Gabriel, then clarify for his companions (may Allah be pleased with them) the correct order in which to recite it.

This is the order in which we now find the completed book. The tradition of going through the Quran in this final order during the month of Ramadan is practiced by Muslims to this day.

Sometimes the revelation of the Quran – which Muslims believe is the last message from Allah to humanity – was revealed in response to specific situations that were occurring in the Prophet's life. Sometimes he would be asked a question by his companions, or mocked by his opponents, and at an appropriate time, a revelation would be 'sent down' to him to address them.

If you read the Quran, you'll notice its discourse sometimes begins with 'Say:…' or 'Tell them….' It's as if we're able to eavesdrop on a conversation between Allah the Almighty and His final Prophet, peace and blessings upon him. It's often helpful, but not always essential, to know to whom those verses are responding.

The Quran was, and still is, primarily transmitted from teacher to student, orally through memorization. However, it was written down during the life of the Prophet, peace and blessings upon him, and collected into one manuscript by his companions after his death. Before the text of the Quran was copied and spread, its authenticity was rigorously corroborated through the companions' memorization.

Muslims take on faith that the Quran is from Allah, the Transcendent. However, it does not take faith for them to know that the Quran we recite today is historically authentic, and is precisely the same as the Quran that was recited on the Prophet's tongue, peace and blessings upon him.

The miracle of the Quran

One of the miraculous things about my exploration of the Quran has been discovering the beautiful coherence of the text when recited in the final order in which we have it today. Each section of revelation the Prophet received bestowed divine wisdom, resolving a pertinent problem He was facing, on one level, and universal wisdom for all of humanity on another level. These pieces of revelation fit seamlessly together, like pieces of a divine jigsaw.

The reason I consider this miraculous is that a passage may start with a chronologically early teaching, move into a chronologically later teaching – which corresponds to an event in the Prophet's life at the time – then move back into a chronologically early teaching, with no break whatsoever in the flow, rhythm, or impact of the message being presented. This happens throughout the Quran – it flows as if it was all written at once, yet it was revealed in such a way that we know that it could not have been.

The more I study the Quran, and see the subtleties of it, the more it's apparent to me that it *actually is* divine revelation from Allah, Who is outside of time and space, to the Prophet. Well, either that or the Prophet had a time machine. In either case, I'm besotted.

Practice didn't make perfect

One might expect that a poet or an author, or a skilled craftsman who has spent years working on his craft and perfecting it, would improve the quality of his output over time. Yet over 23 years, the quality of the Quran did not change or improve. Instead, it remained completely consistent in its outstanding quality. This is another sign that points to its divine nature. The more we study the Quran, the more such signs we see.

Finally, perhaps the most astonishing fact of all is that the Prophet Muhammad, peace and blessings upon him, never learnt to read or write. I've been studying the revelation that he received for the last 20 years, and I don't see an end in sight to its beautiful wisdom.

I've read some of Shakespeare's plays in English, some of Cervantes's in Spanish, and the Quran in Arabic. I have great respect for these inspired authors, but the Quran out-classes them both in every department. Linguistically, stylistically, philosophically, rhythmically, and rhetorically, the Quran is in a league of its own. I've seen nothing else like it in this world. And the man who first articulated it had never read a book.

> *'The superiority of the Quran over the words of man,*
> *is like the superiority of the Creator over His creation.'*[2]
>
> **The Prophet Muhammad, peace and blessings upon him**

It's been said that all the prophets throughout human history, may the peace and blessings of Allah be upon them all, were given impressive miracles. The staff of Moses turned into a snake and the Red Sea parted for him. Jesus could heal the sick, give sight to the blind, and bring the dead back to life. But the greatest miracle, given to the final Messenger, was the Quran.

The difference is that the miracles of the other prophets were visual. One had to be there to see them and appreciate them, or take them on faith. However, the miracle given to the Prophet Muhammad, peace and blessings upon him, had to last until the end of time, as there would be no more prophets after him. That is why the final message and miracle – the Quran – was auditory, so it could be passed on from generation to generation.

The three key messages of the Quran

If we were to look at all of the content of the Quran, to understand its message, we'd find that almost every verse brings us back to three key concepts: there is only One God; many prophets were sent to direct us toward God; and the Afterlife is real.

Allah – 'the God'

'Allah' is the Arabic word for God. In the Arab world, Christians and Jews also refer to God as 'Allah.' The basic formulation of faith for a Muslim is: 'There is no god, except God.' The 'god' with a lower-case 'g' refers to all false deities, including idols and more subtle objects of worship, such as people, material wealth, or our own desires. When we let go of these false deities, all that remains is the One True God – the Source of all that exists.

In the Islamic tradition, there are 99 names of Allah – including Truth, Peace, Love, Mercy, Beauty, Light, Forgiveness, and Wisdom – and all are used in their most absolute form in Arabic. It's made crystal clear from the text of the Quran, as an essential element of faith, that there is One God, Who is beyond time, space, and matter. Any conception of Allah within time, space, and matter is, by definition, not Allah. Allah is the Infinite Intelligence beyond form: the Source of all form. As such, Allah is outside of the human ability to define, or even comprehend.

Allah is not a man

Gender is a property of creation, not the Creator. To associate gender with the Creator is unbefitting, and actually blasphemous in Islam. In the Arabic language there's no gender-neutral pronoun like the English word 'it.' The idea of neutrality is communicated through the masculine pronoun '*huwa*' or 'He.' Allah sometimes uses the royal 'We' or intimate 'Me,' too.

> 'Transcendent is Allah, beyond all that they associate with Him.'[3]
>
> QURAN

The transcendence in this verse includes transcendence beyond gender associations, even though the sentence itself requires the use of the masculine pronoun.

In the early Christian tradition, God was depicted as a man in beautiful images and paintings. This seems to have been an attempt to communicate the stories of the prophets, and of creation, to the uneducated and illiterate masses. Michelangelo's Sistine Chapel ceiling is a shining example of this effort.

Muslims do not attempt to depict Allah, because doing so would necessarily limit Allah, Who is Infinite. Nor do we depict any of the prophets. The beauty of the Prophet Muhammad, peace and blessings upon him, was too great to be captured by a pen. If a fraction of his beauty were to be accurately depicted, humanity could not help but worship his image, instead of Allah: which is the ultimate sin.

The prophets of God

Muslims believe that since the dawn of mankind, every nation, culture, and tribe has been sent revelation from Allah through a prophet or a messenger. All of these prophets delivered the same essential message: believe in Allah and do good.

A saying of the Prophet Muhammad indicates that there were more than 120,000 prophets throughout human history, and only 25 of them are mentioned in the Quran. All prophets are considered impeccable in conduct and free from sin. During the era of any of these prophets, following their path was the 'Islam' of its time, and the best way to find God.

It's assumed that all faithful followers of all the major world religions are following one of these prophets or messengers – even if the transmission of their original message has been distorted over millennia. This is one way in which pluralism of religion and respect for all religions has been built into Islam.

Why Muslims praise prophets

Whenever Muslims say the names of these magnanimous, enlightened prophets and teachers, we show our deep respect and love for them by adding these words: 'May the peace and blessings of Allah be upon him/ her.' This is an exact translation of the Arabic phrase that all Muslims are taught while growing up. In English, it's often abbreviated to 'peace and blessings upon him/her' or simply 'pbuh.'

In writing, it's customary to use the full version of the praise at the start of a book or an article – or at the start of a chapter or a paragraph – and thereafter to use an abbreviation. As I write this book, however, I can't help but type it out in full, almost every time I mention the Prophet Muhammad's blessed name. It helps me connect to his loving essence before speaking about him.

We do something similar for other honored historical figures. For example, for the companions of the Prophet we say, 'May Allah be pleased with her/him.' This is the highest form of adulation given to someone who is not a prophet, and it's usually reserved for a companion or a scholar, or a saint of great importance.

The late boxer Muhammad Ali, one of the greatest sports personalities of all time, famously turned down his place on the Hollywood Walk of Fame. When asked why he would turn down such a great honor, he replied: 'I bear the name of our Beloved Prophet Muhammad (peace be upon him), and it's impossible that I allow people to trample over his name.' In a break with tradition, Hollywood honored Ali even more highly by having his star mounted on the wall of the Kodak Theater instead.

By praising and honoring these enlightened people with these phrases and gestures, we actually raise our *own* status in the eyes of the divine. When we pray for others, angels pray for us. When we praise the Prophet, Allah sends blessings upon us.

The Afterlife

For many people, the message of believing in Allah and doing good is intuitive and seems rational. What then, is the purpose, or need for revelation? One reason is to bestow life-enhancing spiritual wisdom upon us, some of which this book hopes to share. The second reason is to let us know about life after death – something that couldn't possibly be known about without divine revelation.

In order to understand any religion, and benefit from its spiritual wisdom, we must step inside its world without judgment. This is particularly important for the seeker of wisdom because some of the deepest spiritual truths of a religion are embedded within its belief system, which must be understood if they are to be appreciated.

Each religion has its own teachings about the Afterlife. Islam is crystal clear and quite explicit about what happens after death. On every page of the Quran, there's a reference to the Final Day. It's known as the 'Day of Recompense' because we each, as individuals, receive what we earned for ourselves. The final result is either Paradise or Hell. Both are described vividly in the Quran.

Leave judgment to the Judge

The most emphasized elements of the Quran's discourse on the Final Day are that we are each raised as individuals and that no soul shall be wronged or bear the burden of another. No thought, word, or deed is too small to be taken into account.

It's forbidden to assert that a person, or group, will go to Heaven or Hell – including non-Muslims or people of other faiths – because this knowledge is reserved only for Allah. The judgment of the Most Wise is based on imperceptible inner realities, as well as their resulting outward behaviors. For this reason we understand that there's only One True Judge, and it's not me or you. The moment judgment enters the human mind, wisdom leaves.

> 'Is Allah not the wisest of Judges?'[4]
>
> Quran

Rightdoers and wrongdoers

'Out beyond ideas of wrongdoing and rightdoing,
there is a field. I'll meet you there.'

The above is a line from one of my favorite poems by Rumi, the thirteenth-century Persian poet, mystic, and Muslim scholar. The field that he's referring to is the one in which all healing, coaching, spiritual counseling, and transformation takes place.

I've always found it curious that in the West, Rumi is more popular than his primary source for wisdom and insight: the Quran. Much of his poetry elegantly draws on Quranic frames and concepts – when properly understood, his masterpiece the *Maznavi* is considered by some to be the best exegesis of the Quran.

So why is it that today in the West, Rumi's work is so much more popular than the Holy Quran, particularly among non-Muslims? It seems to me that this is largely due to the way his poetry was translated into English. In the line above, for example, the word '*kufr*' is translated as 'wrongdoing.' This is an accurate characteristic of one who does *kufr*, but it's not the most technically accurate translation.

This same word used in the Quran is usually translated as 'disbelief.' This is also slightly inaccurate. '*Kufr*' means 'to cover up, or be in denial of truth' and it implies so much more than being a disbeliever, as you'll discover in Chapter 15.

In a way, the Rumi translation is absolutely brilliant because it gets to the point that the poet was making without the English reader feeling judged and being put in the category of 'disbelief.' The truth is that we don't really know if we're 'rightdoers' or 'wrongdoers.' Similarly, in the Quranic frame, we don't really know if we're 'believers' or 'disbelievers.' Final judgment is reserved for Allah, the Most Wise.

Those who translated Rumi's work – the words of a writer and poet and not the words of Allah Himself – took much greater liberty in interpreting it, which served the general readership by focusing on Rumi's intention, rather than using the most technically precise translation of each word. One is cautious to take such liberties with the Quran, however. All Quran translators aim to translate the Quran as accurately as possible, knowing that we will always, necessarily, fall far short of the magnificence of the original.

There is yet to be a deeply spiritual translation of the Quran that carries the reader along for the spiritual journey we go through when reading it in Arabic. As the Arabic language is so rich, the primary concern of translators has been for technically accurate translations into other languages. This approach is perfectly legitimate, but it comes with a price: the absence of the subtle spiritual connotations of the Quran's words.

In each chapter of Part II of this book, I'll share one important Arabic word and explain its actual meaning, in the hope of giving you a small taste of the sweetness of the spiritual depth of the Quran.

The Quran's teachings are universal

The Quran is for everyone. Every teaching in the Quran applies equally to women and men, unless explicitly stated otherwise in the text, or with some compelling evidence. The fact that the Quran uses the masculine (and neutral) pronoun to refer to Allah, and is addressed primarily to a man (the Prophet), makes it all the more important to highlight this maxim.

It's nonsensical and unbelievable that Allah, the Infinite Intelligence Behind Life who is beyond form and gender, would have an arbitrary preference for one gender over another. All of the teachings presented in this book apply equally to women and men, just as all spiritual teachings in Islam are universal. Women and men are completely equal in their spiritual nature, and differ only in the world of form. Different physical forms do not matter to Allah so much as our spiritual awareness. The Quran says:

> 'Dear People, We created you all from a single man and a single woman, and made you into races and tribes so that you may know one another. In God's eyes, the most honored of you are those who are most conscious of Him: God is all knowing, all aware.[5]

Brilliant and inspiring Muslim women

Despite the fact that Allah's Book views women and men as essentially equal and complementary, sexism continues to exist everywhere in the world. As well as dealing with that, Muslim women also have to deal with stereotypes that imply they are oppressed. This is a misunderstanding, and it seems to be centered around one issue.

Why do you dress like that?

Dalia Mogahed, one of the foremost teachers, speakers, and thought leaders of the Western Muslim community, was recently interviewed on a US talk show and at one point its host cautiously asked her a question that he knew would be on the minds of his viewers: 'Are you oppressed? Why do you dress like that?' He was referring to her *hijab* (headscarf).

I imagine it must be quite frustrating to be an academic and a global thought leader and still need to explain the way you choose to dress. But Ms. Mogahed's answer was honest, unapologetic, and insightful. She wears *hijab*, she told the host, because it's 'an act of devotion to God': 'a commandment' that she should follow. In her view, this is how most Muslim women who wear *hijab* would respond if asked the same question.

Usually when someone makes a sweeping generalization about Muslims, it's wise to call it into question. However, Dalia Mogahed undertook six years of research and conducted the largest, most comprehensive study of the Muslim world to date,[6] and so her generalization about Muslim women was accurate. As Mogahed continued, she focused on what's meant by oppression, i.e. the removal of a person's power.

'What the *hijab* does,' she explained, 'is basically privatize women's sexuality. So what are we saying when we say that taking away, or privatizing, a woman's sexuality is "oppressing her"? What does that mean and say about the source of a woman's power?'

In a classic, cute TV moment, the host responded to the question as if he were a child in a classroom hoping not to disappoint the teacher: 'We're saying a woman is only strong if she's sexy in public?' Gold star, my brother.

What's under the headscarf?

When we finally see beyond the fact that many Muslim women *choose* to wear the headscarf out of devotion, we can come to appreciate them for what their scarf is covering: their brain. When we stop talking about Muslim women and start listening to what they have to say, positive changes happen throughout society.

There are many examples of this throughout Islamic history and civilization, from women whose influence has shaped the world as we know it today. The first university and oldest library in the world, the Qarawiyyin, was founded in Fez, Morocco, in 859 by Fatima al Firhi. In 1236, the ruler of India's powerful Delhi Sultanate was Razia al Din.

The scholar and teacher of imams, jurists, and even the Fifth Umayyad caliph, who ruled from Spain to India, was a Syrian woman called Umm Darda. There are thousands of examples of Muslim women who were the leaders and shapers of Muslim society and Islamic law, centuries before this became prevalent in the West.

The Prophet of empowerment

This empowerment of Muslim women was there at the very starting point of Islam, with the Prophet Muhammad's radical and revolutionary idea that women are actually human beings. He taught that women are the 'twin halves of men' and through Quran revelation, certain rights would be granted to women and made sacred. These included the right to vote, inherit, and own property. It would be well over 1,000 years before that level of autonomy was granted to women in the West.

Muslim women gained full ownership over their money, while husbands were responsible for providing for their wives, even if the women were wealthier. Women had the right to an instant divorce – on returning their dowry – which is something other religions didn't allow. Rather than deny women the right to an education, the Prophet made education compulsory on every Muslim woman. Empowered by these inspiring teachings of the Prophet, the early Islamic era saw Muslim women become scholars, politicians, businesswomen, jurists, and doctors.

The Prophet's first wife, and first love, was our Mother Khadija (may Allah be pleased with her). She was the first Muslim, and the first to believe in his message. She unconditionally supported and loved him. It's perhaps of note that she was also a business leader, his business partner, and his senior by 15 years. And he loved her, more than anyone. Their marriage remains a beautiful example for us all to follow.

The women who preserve Islam

Women are the ones who preserve Islam. It's their loving kindness, caring, and nurturing in the early years of life that teaches a new generation of men and women the essential teachings of Islam. In a more academic sense, those who physically preserve Islam are the scholars of Quran and *hadith*.

A few years ago, Professor Akram Nadwi, a former Oxford research fellow and traditionally trained Muslim scholar, decided to embark on a small project to identify, collect, and record the biographies of female scholars of *hadith* throughout Islamic history. He expected to find a handful of examples and then publish a book on the subject. However, he soon had to readjust his plans.

The resulting work has now reached 40 volumes and is filled with more than 8,000 biographies of Muslim female scholars. Along with theology and jurisprudence, many of them were skilled in calligraphy, philosophy, the sciences, and the liberal arts.

These women didn't just contribute to their societies, they led them. They didn't just live by the *Shariah*, they actively shaped it. In doing so, they had a profound impact on the world as we now know it. It's a real shame that such powerful role models are not household names today.

The women who taught me the Quran

As I was growing up, it was my mother, first and foremost, who taught me the basics of Islam. And as I became more interested in the faith in my late teens, she gifted me a surprising resource that was initially instrumental in connecting me with the message of the Quran.

As she was working her way through a 650-hour home-study program on understanding the Quran, in Urdu, by Pakistan's al-Huda (Guidance) Institute, she gave me an audio series of theirs by Amina Elahi called *A Brief Explanation of the Holy Quran in English*. It didn't seem that brief to me – it came in a large box and was 60 hours long!

I'm currently listening to Ghazala Qureshi's version of the series; the style is very eloquent, and has the right blend of translating the Quran, sharing relevant context, and giving it life through personal examples and reflections. These brilliant Pakistani women had taken it upon themselves not to be taken for granted by the men around them – by educating themselves about the Quran and systematically teaching it.

No one will ever agree with any one person's interpretation of the entire Quran, as it speaks to each of us on an individual level and we each live in a separate reality. But it's wonderful to learn from, and be transformed by, the wisdom of these teachers. Their vision is for the Quran to be in every heart. They certainly succeeded with me. I pray that Allah abundantly rewards these women whose voices came to form part of my conscience, but whom I've never had the honor to meet in person.

I believe that in the modern world, if we are to live up to the Prophet's example, we need this kind of revival of female scholarship in Islam, and to hear the voices of Muslim women, who have always proven to be perfectly capable of speaking for themselves.

Introducing the *Shariah*

One such example of a brilliant Muslim woman speaking for herself in a dignified manner occurred on a chat show in Australia the footage of which went viral. This time, the subject was the *Shariah*.

A politician declared her belief that 'anyone who supports *Shariah* law in this country should be deported.' Fortunately, Yassmin Abdel-Magied, may Allah bless her, was on the panel. She immediately responded to the woman's assertion, asking her: 'Do you even know what *Shariah* law *is*?!'

Excellent question. The *Shariah* is 'the Way' or 'the Path' to Allah. It's the system of morality, spirituality, beliefs, and practices that guides the life of every believer and shows one how to be a faithful Muslim, in any given context. Every Muslim, by this definition, 'supports,' follows, and believes in the *Shariah*.

On a universal level, each of the world's religions has its system of morals, beliefs, and practices. In other words, they each have their '*Shariah.*' If you follow or subscribe to a religion, to a greater or lesser extent, you follow its '*Shariah.*' Believing in, or following, the '*Shariah*' of a religion doesn't conflict with living in a nation state. If anything, it's likely to make one an outstanding citizen.

The content of the Shariah

Just as one of the three dimensions of Islam is to do with external 'practices,' so one element of the *Shariah* is the laws that have been formulated to govern those practices. *Shariah* laws are divided into two categories: laws regarding the five pillars of Islamic worship, and laws that govern the rest of life.

For laws regarding the five pillars of worship, everything is forbidden apart from precisely what's prescribed by the Quran and Sunnah. For the rest of life, everything is allowed except for the few things they explicitly forbid.

The bulk of the *Shariah*'s substance is concerned with how to fulfill the five pillars of Islamic worship. The rest consists of legal matters that are also largely irrelevant to those outside the faith, such as marriage, divorce, funeral rites, food, contract law, and inheritance. The primary objective of the *Shariah* as a whole is the preservation of human life. Its top five overall objectives are the preservation of life, intellect, property, family, and religion.

It's mandated by the *Shariah* that individuals should follow the law of the land in which they live. If that's too difficult

– for example, if one lives in a repressive state where one is prevented from worshipping freely – it then becomes an obligation to migrate.

A lay person cannot derive law

It's highly likely that dangerous misunderstandings and misguidance can result from inaccurate readings, so in the *Shariah* it's forbidden for a lay person – including an avid student like me – to try to deduce *Shariah* rulings or laws based on a direct reading of the scriptural sources.

If I want to learn to pray, for example, I don't do so based on my reading of the Quran and Sunnah. Rather, I learn about it from teachers, and from books written by legitimate scholars that are designed to suit someone with my level of understanding. A well-informed lay person who tries to derive law from the Quran is like a well-intentioned schoolchild attempting open-heart surgery with a kitchen knife.

As much as it's sinful to attempt to derive law from the primary Islamic sources without having the scholastic ability to do so, it's even more sinful to attempt to then implement those laws without a legal system in place, including a judge, judiciary, due process, and the rule of law, among other things.

Even when the Quran does give laws, it's not giving them to you and me. The morals, stories, and spiritual insights are for everyone. Law is for lawyers. No matter how harsh a law given in the Quran sounds on the surface, its correct understanding and implementation is (thankfully) beyond the remit of the general public.

Convert or die?

Historically, people of all faiths were safe in Islamic lands for many reasons, including two crystal-clear Quranic injunctions: 'There is no compulsion in religion'[7] and 'To you, your religion, to me mine.'[8] A non-Muslim would live in Muslim lands as a 'protected citizen,' and would not be judged by the *Shariah* of Islam, but rather by the legal system of his or her own religious community.

A few years ago, I visited the city of Granada in Andalucía in southern Spain. During a walking tour, I discovered that the Jews resident in Spain during the Crusades were rooting for the Muslims, not the Christian crusaders. When the Muslims ruled Andalucía, Jews could safely practice their religion, but when the Christians ruled it, they were made to convert to Christianity under pain of death, so many fled south to modern-day Morocco. Until just over 100 years ago, if you were a Jew suffering persecution, the safest place in the world for you to go was the Islamic lands.

The Quran is not self-contradictory

> 'Will they not think about this Quran? If it had been from anyone other than Allah, they would have found much inconsistency in it.'[9]
>
> Quran

One of the most beautiful things about the Quran is that it doesn't contradict itself, anywhere. In itself, this could be considered miraculous. As human beings we contradict ourselves all the time because our power and intellect are limited. Allah, however, being All-Knowing and Almighty, does not.

The Quran deals with life, death, and the spiritual journey of the human being; it contains legal theory and presents it with precision; it shares deep spiritual truths, along with arguments for the existence of God and the Afterlife – all with arrestingly beautiful logic, inspiring rhetoric, compelling stories, and sheer elegance. Yet, throughout its 6,236 verses, it *never* misplaces a single word.

The fact that – on deep examination – the Quran doesn't contradict itself, forms a basic foundation of Quran interpretation. If one's theory of interpretation of a verse causes a contradiction with other verses, it's clearly an invalid, wrong interpretation. Those who claim, for example, that the Quran permits major sins such as murder, have no way of reconciling this claim with all the verses that forbid it and encourage goodness. A believing Muslim can *never* accept such a contradiction.

The logical, intuitive way believers reconcile apparent contradictions is to take into account the entire text of the Quran, not exclusively the verses whose meanings are ambiguous. When we do this, the apparent contradictions resolve themselves – either through other parts of the text clarifying them, or through consideration of the historical context of the verse in question. In this regard, the Quran says:

> 'It is He who has sent this Scripture down to you [Prophet]. Some of its verses are definite in meaning – these are the cornerstone of the Scripture – and others are ambiguous. The perverse at heart eagerly pursue the ambiguities in their attempt to make trouble and to pin down a specific meaning of their own: only God knows the true meaning. Those firmly grounded in knowledge say, "We believe in it: it is all from our Lord" – only those with real perception will take heed.'[10]

Endless beauty and wisdom

Before we move into Part II of the book, it's important to know that there are endless depths to the beauty, love, and transcendent wisdom of Islam. The biggest challenge in creating this book, therefore, has been to do my best not to limit Islam due to the limitations of my own understanding, intellect and ego.

Every week that passes, I discover ever more beautiful teachings and meanings of verses of the Quran. However, because there are infinite levels of consciousness, and never-ending depths of love and understanding, if I were to continually update this manuscript with every new insight, it would be impossible to ever finish and publish this work.

The times are such that it seems unwise for me to continue my own endless spiritual journey without sharing some of the clarity I've gained thus far. After all, spiritual wisdom is more valuable than treasure, and it only increases when it's given out freely.

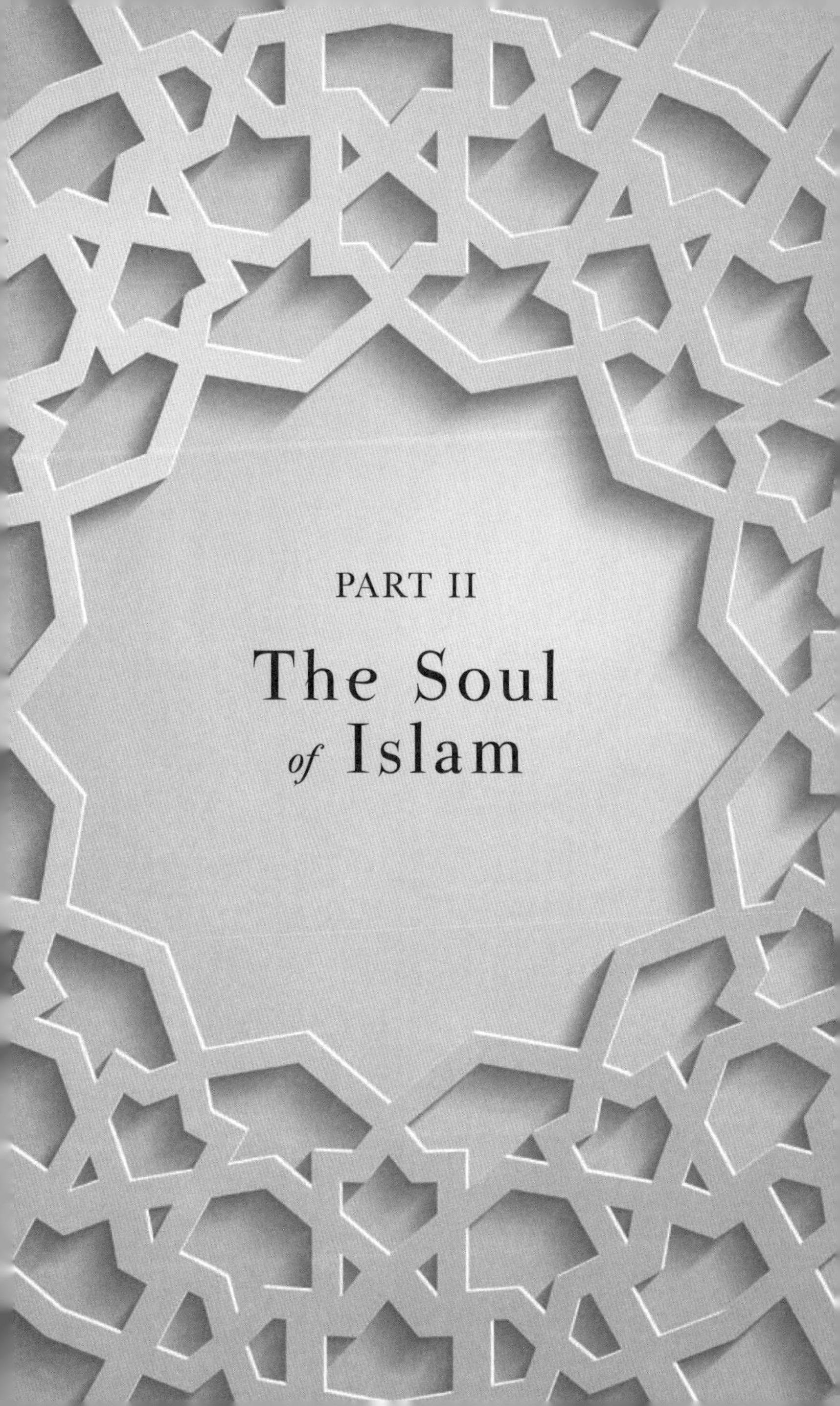

PART II

The Soul *of* Islam

CHAPTER 5

Loving Kindness – the Starting Point

'In the name of Allah,
the Most Kind, the Most Loving.'[1]
QURAN

Before reciting any chapter of the Quran, and before eating or doing anything significant, Muslims begin with the words above. This verse is the starting point of the Quran and it's infused with '*rahma*,' or 'loving kindness.' Without *rahma*, there is no Islam.

In English the word *rahma* is often translated as 'mercy,' which although accurate, doesn't carry the full meaning of the Arabic word. It also means 'graciousness, benevolence, kindness, love, beneficence, and compassion.' I generalize all of these to mean 'loving kindness,' on the understanding that it's a universal, divine, spiritual form of love. There are 14 commonly used words for 'love' in Arabic and 36 different words used in the Quran for what we would call 'love' in

English. The word *rahma* is a profound kind of love that's universal, yet intense.

Arabic words are generally based on a 'root' that uses three letters to define the original underlying meaning of the word. From the same root, 'r-h-m,' we derive the word for 'womb' and the word for 'loving kindness.' The implication is that *rahma* is the kind of love a mother has for her child.

The starting point of the Quran

The opening chapter of the Quran, which is contained within a single page, is a prayer called *Surah al-Fatiha*, or 'The Opener.' Its seven verses are said to contain the blessings and teachings of the entire Quran. In many ways, *Al-Fatiha* is the be-all and end-all of our faith. It doesn't just open the Quran – it opens our hearts to the guidance contained within the Quran. It doesn't matter how advanced we become in our studies, we always come back to this, in every prayer:

> 'In the name of Allah, the Most Kind, the Most Loving;
> All gratitude and praise is due to Allah, Lord of all the worlds;
> The Most Kind, the Most Loving,
> Master of the Day of Recompense,
> You alone we worship; You alone we ask for help.
> Guide us to the Straight Path
> The path of those you have blessed;
> those who incur no anger, and who have not gone astray.
> Ameen.'[2]

Muslims who pray five times a day recite this first page of the Quran from memory at least 17 times in a single day. Love is thus infused into our daily lives and is inseparable from our spiritual journey.

From the outset of the Quran, and at the beginning of every prayer, it's made clear that Allah is *ar-Rahman* (the Most Kind and Merciful) and *ar-Raheem* (the Most Benevolent and Loving). Both words are absolute forms of the word *rahma*; however, *ar-Raheem* is an even more intense form. In a beautiful narration, the Prophet, peace and blessings upon him, reported:

'Allah has divided "rahma" *into 100 parts. One part has been given to all of creation and He kept 99 parts to himself.'*[3]

Muslim scholars say that this 1 percent of love comes from Allah's name *ar-Rahman* (the Most Kind, Most Merciful), and encompasses all the love you've ever known, all the love that all of humanity – past, present, and future – has ever known, and all the love that's ever been expressed between any animal and its offspring, as well as between all those life forms known to us, and those unknown.

It's said that the other 99 percent of love comes from Allah's name *ar-Raheem* (the Most Benevolent, Most Loving), and is reserved for use by Him on the Day of Recompense.

To further highlight this quality of the divine, one of the most well-known and commonly memorized chapters of the Quran is the *Surah ar-Rahman*, or 'the Most Merciful.' The emphasis of this chapter, as its title suggests, is the attribute of Divine Mercy. Our ultimate example of how to live a loving, merciful, benevolent life is found in the Prophet Muhammad, peace and blessings upon him. The Quran says:

> 'Indeed you [Prophet] were not sent, but as a mercy [rahma] for all the worlds.'[4]

The more we can embody the quality of *rahma*, the more we're following the example of the Prophet, peace and blessings upon him. Using different words for love, kindness, and gentleness, there are hundreds, perhaps thousands, of sayings of the Prophet Muhammad, peace and blessings upon him, that encourage us to be more loving and kind toward creation.

The starting point of Prophetic sayings

The first saying of the Prophet, peace and blessings upon him – which is taught to all students in traditional *madrassas* (Islamic schools) before they can study any of the others – is known as the 'Saying of *Rahma*.' This is because a derivation of this word is used five times in this short, powerful Prophetic statement:

> *'Those who are loving, are loved by the Most Loving; so love those on Earth and those in Heaven will love you.'*[5]

There's wisdom in teaching this Prophetic saying first because it reminds the teacher to be merciful, kind, and loving to the new student, so as not to put them off. Similarly, the student must show mercy, patience, and understanding toward the teacher, especially at the beginning of their long journey together into the beauty of sacred knowledge. The deeper wisdom is that if the student's journey ends prematurely, he or she will at least receive the gift of these beautiful Prophetic words, which form the foundation of the faith of Islam.

Below are just a few of the hundreds of teachings of the Prophet, peace and blessings upon him, that encourage us to be more loving and kind to each other.

'Love for humanity what you love for yourself.'[6]

'Wish for your neighbor what you wish for yourself.'[7]

'Do not belittle any act of kindness, even that of greeting your brother with a cheerful countenance.'[8]

'Whoever is kind to a woman is honorable; whoever humiliates a woman is cruel.'[9]

'A good deed done to an animal is like a good deed done to a human being, while an act of cruelty to an animal is as bad as cruelty to a human being.'[10]

The benevolent, merciful actions of the Prophet, peace and blessings upon him, are too numerous to list here. Indeed, it wouldn't be an exaggeration to say that his *every* action was loving, benevolent, and kind. I'd like to share a couple of small illustrations of this, giving you a brief glimpse into the reality of his love for creation.

One time, as the Prophet, peace and blessings upon him, sat reciting the Quran, a cat fell asleep on his robe. When the time came to leave, rather than disturb the animal from its slumber, he cut off a portion of his robe and quietly walked away.

On another occasion he was praying in the full bowing position, with his forehead on the ground, when his grandchildren, Hassan and Hussain – may Allah be pleased with them – ran into the room and jumped on his back. Rather than reprimanding the children, his response was simply to prolong his bowing, allowing them to continue playing.

The Prophet, peace and blessings upon him, emphasized kindness to women and children, saying:

> *'The most complete in faith are those who are best in character and kindest to their families.'*[11]

We've barely scratched the surface of the Islamic imperative to love humanity, our neighbors, our friends, and our families. No matter how loving and kind we are to others, it pales in comparison to the love and kindness demonstrated by the

Prophet, peace and blessings upon him, to those around him. His love for humanity was powerful enough to establish a religion that's still followed by more than a billion people more than 1,400 years later.

The Prophet's love – peace and blessings upon him – was a reflection of his acknowledgment of the grace that the Most Loving is bestowing on all of us in every moment. Every breath and every heartbeat is Allah's love being manifest into our lives. The very fact that we're even thinking, means we're experiencing Allah's love for us.

Loving people from the Inside-Out

All of these teachings seem like wonderful ideas, and because I'm a nice guy, I lived most of my life thinking that I was fulfilling them by default. It was only after discovering the Inside-Out understanding that I realized just how egotistical I was, and how much more potential for love there is inside me.

The Inside-Out understanding creates enormous space for us to insightfully improve our character, which is the essence of Islam. Through removing a misunderstanding about the way reality works, we effortlessly become more loving, compassionate, and kind when we're with our families, no matter how difficult they appear to be.

The first time I explained the Inside-Out Paradigm to a couple who are good friends of mine, the wife immediately said something that completely threw me: 'What about love?

Surely love doesn't just come from thoughts?! I'm so in love with my husband and that has to be coming from somewhere deeper than just the way I'm thinking!'

I knew there was something 'off' about her analysis, but as I didn't want to seem heartless, I kept quiet. I did, however, deeply reflect on her question. The truth is, when I first discovered the Inside-Out, I had to do a lot of 'recalculating' because it's a completely different way of seeing life. Thankfully, most of this happened through insightful realization, rather than through any hard work on my part.

Like my friends – may Allah bless this couple and give them the best in this life and the next – I'd literally spent my whole life believing that being with loved ones is what makes you feel loved. And you can tell who your loved ones are by the way you feel about them. If you make me feel happy and loved, I'll give you my time. If you make me feel angry and sad, I'm staying clear of you. There is, however, a terribly illogical flaw in this thinking that was making me a much less loving person than I could be.

Taking the target off your back

Valda Monroe, my friend and teacher, once told me a cute story about her and her husband Keith that summarizes just about every dispute I've ever had with a family member. It also points toward the logic and beautiful wisdom of the Inside-Out Reality.

There was once a pile of wood in front of Valda and Keith's house, and to Valda, it looked quite ugly. She'd asked Keith many times to move the woodpile, but he never did, because in his view, although it was unsightly, it was out of harm's way.

One day Valda arrived home, looked at Keith, and was filled with feelings of love and adoration for her amazing husband. *I'm so lucky and blessed to have such a wonderful man in my life*, she thought. As she hugged him tightly, she caught a glimpse of the woodpile in the background. Instantly, her head started filling up with less-than-loving thoughts about Keith: *He's so stubborn! Why doesn't he just move it?!* She was instantly feeling frustrated with him.

In that moment, Valda had a sudden insight: *There's no way that Keith can possibly be the source of my feelings!* One minute she was completely lovey-dovey toward him, and the next she was filled with frustration. The only thing that had changed from one moment to the next was her *thoughts* about Keith and the woodpile. Nothing had actually changed in the outside world. In fact, Keith was standing there in exactly the same way as he had been just a few moments earlier. All of this had been going on inside Valda's head. When she had that realization, she said to Keith: 'I'm going to be on your team a lot more from now on.'

Keith was surprised to hear this: 'Weren't you already on my team?' he asked. With deep honesty, Valda insightfully replied: 'No, I don't think I have been on your team as much as I could have been.'

Later, Valda said that it was as if she'd spent all those years with Keith without realizing she'd placed a target on his back. Every time she felt negative and was simultaneously thinking about Keith, she'd assumed that her negative feelings were coming *from* him. To her, it looked as if there was something she had to do about 'him,' in order to make the feelings go away.

If he would just move the woodpile, she must have reckoned, *that would make me feel so much better and I would love him so much more.* Every time she felt positive and was simultaneously thinking about Keith, she must also have assumed that her positive, loving feelings were coming from him. The truth is that all of her feelings were always coming from the power of thought.

The One True Source of Love

What a relief it must have been in that household when Valda realized that she no longer needed to hold Keith to account for the way she was feeling – whether that was positive or negative. What a relief it is for all of us when other people stop holding us to account for the way *they* feel. And what a blessing we become for others when we stop treating *them* as the source of our good or bad feelings.

In reality, our most deeply loving feelings have always been coming from the Source of Love: *Ar-Rahman*. When we're Outside-In, we all make the innocent mistake of attributing our loving feelings to the one we love, instead of to the One Source of Love – Allah.

The moment we notice this subtle but pervasive shift in perspective, we automatically become much more loving. It's really difficult to be loving toward someone if you genuinely believe they are the cause of your anger, hurt, or sadness. The instant you realize that they were *never* the cause of any of that, you automatically become a lot more able to be loving toward them, if you wish.

This doesn't mean that they didn't do those bad things – it means that your feelings didn't come from the bad things they did, but from *the way you think* about those bad things in this moment. The moment we take our feelings off the person and what they did, we're able to see the relationship much more clearly. Moving a woodpile suddenly becomes a simple matter of logistics, not a reason for a fight.

I've always thought of the Prophetic saying 'love those on Earth and those in Heaven love you' as a command. That's one valid interpretation of it; however, there's a deeper spiritual meaning here too: the fact that you're feeling love for humanity *means* that you're experiencing Allah loving you.

The very love that you feel for humanity comes from Allah, the Source of Love, through the vehicle of thought. The fact that you can only feel thought is a true blessing, and an expression of Allah's love for you. When you intensely love your most beloved, Allah is blessing you with that feeling of love, and it's coming to you via the spiritual gift of thought.

The loving way to approach Islam

Allah, the Most Loving, the Most Kind, has made loving kindness the starting point of all of our study of Islam. It's as though we're being taught, by the divine, the most beneficial way to approach religion and the sacred Quran: through Love. This must be our methodology if we want true guidance – to look at Islam with eyes of love and seek within it, true love. For our objective is to be with Allah. And Allah *is* 'Love.'

This starting point is of great significance. You can't gain guidance by studying misguidance. You can't gain understanding by studying misunderstanding. You can't gain wisdom by studying ignorance. You can't see the light by searching in the darkness. You can't find love by researching hatred. And you can't understand Islam by studying terrorism.

Every now and then, I become very concerned when I see on the news a political pundit, or a self-proclaimed 'expert' on Islam, claiming that Islam is a religion of terror, not love. Then something occurs to me, which brings relief and clarity. If we ask the 'expert' to tell us what the first page of the Quran says, without looking on Google, despite their studies, they'll be unable to answer the question. And yet, literally every single Muslim who prays knows the first page of the Quran by heart, and recites it every day. This is a deeply significant fact.

The essence of the Quran

I've come to believe that every human being would benefit immensely from a careful reading of the first chapter of the Quran – the *Surah al-Fatiha*, 'The Opener' – for the following reasons:

- It may be challenging for people to read the entire 600 pages of the Quran, but *Surah al-Fatiha* has only seven verses.
- *Surah al-Fatiha* contains within it the message of the entire Quran. The rest of Allah's Book is said to be a divine commentary on this first chapter.
- The seven beautiful verses of *Surah al-Fatiha* form the bulk of the substance of a believer's faith. This is what we all recite and reflect on deeply, every day.
- Most outsiders haven't noticed it, because they don't deeply reflect and pray on it, but the last line of this prayer contains a beautifully humble but powerful condemnation of the kind of misguidance that, in its grossest form, leads to murder and terrorism.
- It's a beautiful, universal prayer for guidance that can only be of benefit to the one who reads it; it's designed to keep us all on the 'Straight Path' toward Allah: the Path of Love, Truth, Kindness, Compassion, Benevolence, and Peace.

Part of the beauty of the Quran, and of Islam, is that the most advanced practices and teachings are the very first ones we learn. The starting point and end point are one. It doesn't matter how spiritual we become, and how much insight we're blessed with, we never leave the prayer we learn when we first become Muslims. Rather, we're invigorated by it. If we misunderstand or ignore the first page of the Quran, we're lost, despite all our knowledge. Any exploration of Islam is pointless without the starting point.

May Allah protect us from being among those who miss the starting point and essence of Islam. May Allah bless all the readers of this book to be among those who are guided to the Straight Path.

I'll end this chapter in the way it began, with the most beautiful and significant of prayers from the Quran:

> 'In the name of Allah, the Most Kind, the Most Loving;
> All gratitude and praise is due to Allah, Lord of all the worlds;
> The Most Kind, the Most Loving,
> Master of the Day of Recompense,
> You alone we worship; You alone we ask for help.
> Guide us to the Straight Path
> The path of those you have blessed;
> those who incur no anger, and who have not gone astray.
> Ameen.'[12]

CHAPTER 6

Knowledge – the Path of the Seeker

'Whoever follows a path in the pursuit of knowledge, Allah eases for them a path to Paradise.'[1]

The Prophet Muhammad,
peace and blessings upon him

This is a noble journey on which you're embarking – into the heart of what it means to be human. The pursuit of true spiritual knowledge and wisdom is one of the most praiseworthy actions in which we can invest our time and energy. This type of knowledge benefits us far more than any material gain.

The first revelation

The Prophet Muhammad, peace and blessings upon him, had always been known for his trustworthiness and sincerity. With this sincerity, before receiving any revelation from the divine, he would go and sit in a cave on Mount Hira, in the middle of the Arabian desert, for hours on end each day. He was on a spiritual quest, seeking the same thing you are.

Eventually, when his mind was quiet and his heart ready, at a time of Allah's choosing, the Archangel Gabriel, upon whom be peace, came to him and the first words of the Quran were revealed to him:

'Read!'

As he was illiterate and had never read a book, the Prophet, peace and blessings upon him, replied, *'I cannot read.'*

Again, he heard the message: 'Read!'

Again, he replied, *'I cannot read.'*

The third time, he was able to recite, and the whole passage was revealed to him:

> 'Read! In the name of your Lord, who created;
> Created mankind from a morsel.
> Read! Your Lord is Most Generous,
> Who taught by the pen;
> Taught mankind what they did not know.'[2]

After this profound experience, the Prophet Muhammad, peace and blessings upon him, was overwhelmed by shock and awe. He ran home to his wife and first love, Khadija, may Allah be pleased with her; when he arrived, he was rushed, flustered, out of breath, and shaking. All he could say to Khadija was: *'Cover me! Cover me!'*

He collapsed, and later awoke, more calm. He said to his wife: *'I am afraid, dear Khadijah. I am afraid that I will be harmed.'*

Khadija already knew that her husband was special, and rumors had been going around that a true prophet was coming. She reassured him, in the words of a loving wife:

> *'There is no reason for you to feel any kind of fear or worry. Do not be sad. God would never embarrass a servant like you. I know that you always speak the truth. You perform duties that have been given to you and safeguard that which has been entrusted to you.*
>
> *'You interact closely with your relatives. You treat your neighbors in a very kind and caring manner. You help the poor. You open your doors to strangers and entertain them as guests. You help the community during disasters and tribulations. So, persevere. By God, I hope that you are this community's prophet.'*[3]

The word of God

That day literally changed the world, and the entire course of human history. One man, on his own, sitting in a cave, seeking God. More than 1,400 years later, the wisdom he received is still as deep, beautiful, and relevant as ever. We're on the same path that he was. And although the Archangel Gabriel may not come to us directly, to give us guidance in our own language, we're blessed to be able to benefit from what was revealed to the Prophet Muhammad, peace and blessings upon him,

As I explained earlier, Muslims believe that the Quran is literally the word of Allah, Who is outside of time, space, and matter. And we believe that Allah communicated this message to us, in much the same way that messages have been communicated to other prophets and messengers since the dawn of humanity, among them Abraham, Moses, and Jesus, peace and blessings upon them all.

I believe that the Quran is communication from the Universal Intelligence Behind Life. However, benefiting from it is not restricted to believers. Anyone whose heart is open can benefit from the Light of the Quran and the teachings of the Prophet, peace and blessings upon him. Allah says in the Quran:

> 'There has come to you, from Allah, a Light and a Clear Book by which Allah guides whoever follows His good pleasure in the ways of peace, and brings them forth from the darkness into the Light, by His permission, and guides them to a Straight Path.'[4]

The aim of Islam is to take the sincere spiritual seeker from the darkness of ignorance into the light of divine knowledge. It's no surprise, then, that the very first word of the Quran is an imperative: 'Read!'

Seeking knowledge – a sacred duty

'Seeking knowledge is an obligation for every Muslim man and Muslim woman.'[5]

THE PROPHET MUHAMMAD, PEACE AND BLESSINGS UPON HIM

There are so many hundreds of beautiful Prophetic sayings that point us toward the virtues of studying and seeking knowledge. During the peak of Islamic civilization, from the eighth to the thirteenth centuries, these teachings were the inspiration for the great Muslim scientists, artists, philosophers, and thinkers who made groundbreaking discoveries and furthered civilization with their knowledge.

For the most part, these pioneers were all traditionally trained scholars, and their pursuit of knowledge in diverse fields of specialization, from the sciences to the humanities, was based on a desire to unify them and explore how they all point us back to Allah. Many of these great intellectuals were polyglots, by virtue of their education system.

In Islam, education is not a right. It's an obligation. My father wasn't just being strict with me while I was growing up – he was enforcing on me one of the greatest virtues of the entire religion: to gain knowledge. When the young Pakistani girl Malala Yousafzai was shot in the face by the Pakistani Taliban in 2012, recovered and then returned immediately to school, it wasn't just a grand act of heroism. It was a fundamental requirement of her faith: fulfilling her duty to become educated, even in the face of violent, ignorant opposition.

'Studying together for an hour during the night
is better than spending the whole night in devotions.'[6]

The Prophet Muhammad, peace and blessings upon him

In Islam, all knowledge is considered sacred, as all knowledge ultimately leads to a deeper knowledge of Allah – the purpose of life. Each chapter of the Quran is made up of 'verses,' but in Arabic these verses are called '*ayahs*,' which literally means 'signs.' It's said that Allah has revealed two books containing these *ayahs* (signs), which point us toward His Presence. The first is the Quran. The second is the rest of the Universe. Exploring the Universe is a way of deepening our knowledge of Allah.

'When Allah wishes good for someone,
He bestows upon him understanding in religion.'[7]

The Prophet Muhammad, peace and blessings upon him

Not all knowledge is equal, however. 'Beneficial knowledge' is considered praiseworthy and intrinsically valuable, whereas 'harmful knowledge' is not. There's also a distinction between breadth of knowledge, which requires deliberate study, and depth of insight, which comes from within.

Breadth of knowledge and depth of insight

'The companions once asked the Prophet, peace and blessings upon him, "What is the best action for a person?" He answered, "To know Allah."'[8]

There are two distinct forms of knowledge: knowledge that can be learnt from books and teachers, and true spiritual wisdom, which can only come from within. The latter occurs through insight, and only when Allah chooses to bless us with it.

When it comes to religious knowledge, the hope and aim is that by systematically studying certain texts with a qualified teacher, and by engaging in certain practices such as the five daily prayers, additional night prayers, and other practices, the student gains spiritual insight. These spiritual gains are common, but there's no guarantee that they will occur.

In my spare time, one of my favorite things to do is memorize the Quran. Times have changed since the old Maulvi Saab days; my teacher today is a cool Moroccan brother who's become a good friend. He's a *hafidh* – one who has memorized the Quran – and is full of spiritual light. He's also surprisingly young for one so accomplished – may Allah continue to bless him with insight and make him a leading scholar and light for humanity.

I take a class every week, where I sit with my teacher for a few hours, learning to correctly recite a new section of the Quran. When I can recite it in precisely the correct manner,

I'm sent home and the aim is that by the next session, I've committed that section to memory. Each week, by the grace of Allah, the breadth of my knowledge increases, measurably.

However, that isn't the greatest benefit I personally receive from this time invested. The greatest benefit is that by spending many hours with these 'signs' that point toward Allah, I'm occasionally, through no effort on my part, and completely unexpectedly, overwhelmed with insight.

This is the greatest blessing I've ever known. It always comes with a delicious feeling of depth, gratitude, and awe toward the One who blessed me with it. It can bring me to tears, and frequently does. It's not the knowledge itself that counts, but the moment that the knowledge 'hits' me. *That* is insight, and it is, in my experience, the greatest benefit and blessing of studying spiritual scriptures.

'On the Day of Judgment, the ink of a scholar will outweigh the blood of a martyr.'[9]

THE PROPHET MUHAMMAD, PEACE AND BLESSINGS UPON HIM

Insightful transformation from the Inside-Out

Breadth of knowledge requires us to understand, memorize, and then apply it. Insight transforms us automatically, from the Inside-Out. We don't need to 'apply' an insight. Insight is Allah bestowing spiritual wisdom upon us. Allah does the work, and we're changed for the better.

We don't need to be studying to receive insight. It can come at any time, during any activity, and in any form. It's almost a cliché to say that creatives, artists, and entrepreneurs have their best ideas while in the shower, or out walking in a park. These are insights that come from Allah, from within their consciousness. However, the greatest of all insights are those that lead to a deeper knowledge of one's self, and therefore of Allah.

'The one who knows himself, knows his Lord.'[10]

The Prophet Muhammad, peace and blessings upon him.

I think of the Inside-Out Paradigm as the 'Insight-Generator' because the more we recognize the True Source of our experience, the more we're open to insight. Sydney Banks had insight about the nature of the self and Allah when he realized the Three Principles. Many of my friends have had insights while listening to Banks speak, much as I do when I'm memorizing and reciting the Quran.

I had insight about myself and Allah when, during that coaching session all those years ago, I instantly and effortlessly dropped all of my limited thinking about being divorced. Insight is a real phenomenon, and the 'people of insight' are mentioned and praised several times in the Quran.

Sources of knowledge

'The scholars are the heirs of the prophets.
The prophets did not leave behind money or coins,
rather they left behind knowledge,
so whoever takes it has taken a great share.'[11]

The Prophet Muhammad, peace and blessings upon him

Gaining knowledge requires a good book, a good teacher, and a good student. The 'book' may be the Quran itself, but this raises a question: who do we study it with? Can anyone stand up and claim to be a 'scholar' of the Quran and teach other people their interpretation? In this age of the internet, people certainly try.

However, there's a huge difference between learning Islam from one of the inheritors of the Prophet, peace and blessings upon him, and learning it from Google. In the modern world, this difference has become quite drastically apparent.

In Islam, there's no 'church' in the way that there's a Catholic or a Protestant church. No one is considered to be, by position or status alone, more holy than anyone else. We've all been given a soul, and can do with it what we wish. However, there's still a form of hierarchy in Islam, and it's one based primarily on knowledge.

If someone has dedicated their life to gaining Islamic knowledge – such as learning the methodology of Quran interpretation, which requires a deep knowledge of logic, rhetoric, linguistics, and grammar – then they may earn the highly honored status of being a 'scholar' of '*tafsir*,' or Quran exegesis.

The distinction, however, is that their status is based on meritocracy and knowledge. Anyone can become a scholar if they're willing to do the requisite study, with a legitimate teacher. A person does not become a scholar because we think they're knowledgeable – they do so because their teachers and institutions have certified them as experts in certain areas of religious knowledge.

'This knowledge is religion, so consider from whom you take your religion.'[12]

The Prophet Muhammad, peace and blessings upon him

How to find the perfect teacher

I spent many years of my life searching for the perfect teacher of Islam – a scholar deeply grounded in the Islamic sources who'd be able to walk me through everything I needed to know about contemporary life. All of it taught step-by-step, in an easy-to-learn format, and preferably on a schedule that fitted in with my daily routine.

That never quite happened. I've been blessed to know, and befriend, several legitimate scholars of Islam, and I've learnt, over time, that there's a much more realistic and practical approach: to see everyone as our teacher.

'Wisdom is the lost property of the believer,
so wherever he finds it, he takes it.'[13]

The Prophet Muhammad, peace and blessings upon him

I respect all scholars for their knowledge, and will show them all the etiquette required in order to benefit from them and be of benefit to them. However, in order to do this, I realized two things: #1: it's impossible for me to agree with everything a scholar says, because we live in separate realities; and #2: it's possible for me to benefit from anyone, regardless of their knowledge level, or whether or not I agree with them, if I'm open to it.

With this understanding, I'm able to learn from a great variety of scholars, some of whom I might have been put off by when I was younger and more eager to find the 'perfect' teacher. A wise friend once told me that the ramblings of a drunken man on the street can bring you more benefit than the most erudite, knowledgeable scholar. It depends on the sincerity in your heart and the truth on their tongue. Wisdom comes from within your own soul.

You may have wondered whether I'm a legitimate scholar of the religion of Islam. The answer is no, I'm not a scholar. I'm a student of knowledge and a seeker of wisdom. There are many brilliant and erudite scholars of Islam at whose feet

I learn, and on whose knowledge I depend. If they contradict anything in this book, trust them over me. Just beware that not everyone standing on a (digital) pulpit has earned the right to be there. And know that when you hear truth, it touches your soul, and you will know it, without doubt.

Prophetic words for the seeker of wisdom

By virtue of the fact that you're reading this book, you're actively seeking the highest form of knowledge: spiritual knowledge. For that, may you find it, and be eternally rewarded. To encourage you on this journey, and to encourage you to continue reading, the following is a gift – some beautiful encouragement from the Prophet Muhammad, peace and blessings upon him, which can be both an aid and a source of delight as you continue on this noble path.

The Prophet Muhammad, peace and blessings upon him, said:

> *'Pursue knowledge, for pursuing it is reverence to God, seeking it is devotion, studying it with others is glorification, searching it out is striving in the path of God, teaching it to one who lacks knowledge is charity, bestowing it freely on those worthy of it brings proximity [to God].*
>
> *'[Knowledge] is an intimate companion in solitude, a friend in retreat, and a guide to religion; it heartens one in ease and difficulty; it is a vizier among noble*

companions and a close friend among strangers;
it is a guiding light on the path to heaven.

'God elevates people [through knowledge], making them leaders, lords, and guides who are followed on the path of excellence; they are exemplars in goodness, their traces are followed closely and their comportment is closely noted; the angels seek out intimate friendship with them, and with their wings stroke them; every [creature] of the field or the desert seeks forgiveness for them, even the fish and the sea snakes of the oceans, the wild animals of dry land and its grazing beasts, [even] the heavens and its stars.

'All this because knowledge is the life of the heart [protecting it] from blindness, the light of eyesight [protecting it] from darkness, and the strength of the body [sustaining it] from weakness.

'The servant attains through it the stations of the upright and the loftiest degrees. Reflection on it equals fasting, and studying it with others equals devotional prayers through the night.

'Through it God is obeyed, by it He is worshipped, by it His unity is affirmed, by it He is lauded, and by it He is approached with piety. By it family ties are maintained, and by it the lawful and unlawful are known.

'Knowledge is the leader, and deeds are his followers. Those who will be happy are inspired by it, and those who will be miserable are kept from it.'[14]

CHAPTER 7

Spreading Peace – the First Commandment

'Peace be with you.'

Every single Muslim, ever

As-Salam Alaikum ('Peace be with you') is a greeting, and a prayer, given by every Muslim. *As-Salam* is one of Allah's 99 names, and it means 'Peace.' Allah literally *is* Peace. An 'Islam' without 'Peace' is as impossible and nonsensical as an Islam without 'Allah.'

Muslims end each of their five daily prayers by turning their faces to the right, then to the left, and saying, 'May the Peace, Love, and Blessings of Allah be with you.' This is an address to the angels – who are believed to be on our right and left sides – and, symbolically, to the whole of creation that surrounds us. Then a Prophetic invocation is made: 'Allah, you are Peace; from You comes all Peace; You are Blessed, the Possessor of all Glory and Honor.'

The words 'Islam' and 'Muslim' come from the Arabic root word *salama*, which means 'to be peaceful/safe/protected.' The verbal noun of the fourth form of this word is 'Islam,' which is a peaceful acceptance or surrender.

'Islam' is the profound state of inner peace that can come only from accepting and surrendering to '*what is*.' Muslims believe that 'what is' is the will of Allah, the Most Powerful. The word 'Muslim' is the active participle of 'Islam.' In other words, the Muslim is the one who finds peace by surrendering to, and accepting, what is. By this linguistic definition and spiritual understanding, every sincere spiritual seeker, regardless of his or her chosen path or belief system, is attempting to be a true Muslim.

Seeing 'what is' from the Inside-Out

The beauty and power of the Inside-Out Paradigm is that it gives us a clear, logical way to see 'what is' from 'what is not'; to see truth from falsehood; to see reality from illusion. When we're aware that our experience is always coming from the divine power of thought in the moment, we're aligned with 'what is.'

Therefore we are, spiritually, living Islam. When we pretend that our feelings could be coming from something other than Allah, via thought in the moment, we're in denial of what is. This denial is where the ego begins, and ends.

The Prophet of peace

The focus of life for a Muslim is to embody the divine quality of *salam*, or peace. That is, to be at peace within themselves, at peace with the Creator, and as a result, at peace with all of creation. The opposite of this is to be in a state of conflict: at war within one's self, at war with the Creator, and at war with creation.

This is demonstrated by the following saying of the Prophet, peace and blessings upon him. It's known as the 'Saying of *Salam*' because it begins and ends with *salam*, and was reported by a man named Abdallah ibn Salam, may Allah be pleased with him. He was a rabbi and one of the leaders of the Jews of Medina. He said:

> *'When I heard that the Prophet had come to Medina, I went to see him. As soon as I saw him, I recognized that his face was not the face of a liar.'*

It's notable that just by witnessing the face of the beloved Messenger, peace and blessings upon him, this rabbi instantly became a Muslim. I imagine this would be the case for any sincere seeker who was blessed to see a truly enlightened teacher. Just by looking at the beauty of the Prophet's face, peace and blessings upon him, which is said to have been filled with overwhelming spiritual light, Abdallah ibn Salam instantly knew that this was an honest man, and so he must have been true in his claim to be a prophet of God.

As a point of interest, in every physical description I've ever read of the Prophet, peace and blessings upon him, the narrator at some point describes him as simply the most beautiful person, or thing, that they'd ever laid eyes on. I believe this is due to both his physical and his spiritual beauty.

Abdallah ibn Salam continued:

> *'I went over to greet him and the first words that came out of his mouth were: "Dear People: spread peace, feed the hungry, be good to your families, pray at night while people sleep, and you'll enter Paradise in Peace."'*[1]

These four commandments, addressed to humanity, summarize the essential teachings of the religion of Islam; and the reward promised to those who follow them is eternal peace. Part of the beauty and wisdom of the Prophet's advice – peace and blessings upon him – is that he would often speak in order of importance. In other words, these four commandments are in the exact order of their spiritual importance. To spread peace comes first.

On another occasion, the Prophet, peace and blessings upon him, said:

'Do you want me to point out to you something that will enable you to love each other? Spread peace among each other.'[2]

As well as meaning 'peace' the word *salam* can be defined as 'the absence of harm.' For Muslims, it's such a blessing to have this as a greeting directed toward every human being we meet. Saying 'Peace be with you' means 'I wish you no harm' and 'I want nothing but good for you.' If someone says this, and then attempts to harm the person they've just greeted, they were quite literally lying when they spoke. Lying is, of course, a sin in Islam, which would be added to the sin of attempting to harm the person in the first place.

The Prophet, peace and blessings upon him, defined a Muslim as follows:

'The Muslim is the one from whose hands and tongue people are safe.'[3]

By this Prophetic definition, if people are not safe from an individual's hands and tongue, that person is not a true Muslim.

'Islam means da peace'

My friends and I have an ongoing joke: while you almost never see people on TV saying sensible things about Islam, every now and then there will be an old 'Uncle Gee' from the

Indian subcontinent who, in thickly accented English, tries to articulate where Islam stands. The best he'll be able to muster is some variation of 'Islam means da' Peace!'

This is tragically ironic because, even though he can't keep up with the debates taking place in his second or third language, he's actually right. In essence, the religion teaches nothing but how to be a better, more peaceful, more loving human being. The problem is that this just doesn't sound convincing coming from someone who may be a scholar in his country of origin, but whose wisdom is lost in translation.

Muslims in the West don't stand a chance of convincing non-Muslims that terrorism is completely forbidden in their religion, when all a terrorist needs to do is kill more people, then wave his hands in the air and say, 'Hey everyone, I'm a Muslim!'

The quiet whispers of truth spoken by hundreds of millions of believing Muslims can't drown out the loud shouts of *'Allahu Akbar'* before a terrorist kills someone. Even though, in the religion of Islam, there's no justification whatsoever for murder, every time the terrorists do this, more people look upon Muslims and our religion with suspicion.

The rope that binds together the lie that Islam permits murder is the use of the term 'Islamic terrorism.' Think about what this literally means. 'Islam,' the name of a religion, is being used as an adjective to describe the grave sin of mass murder. If we say there's an 'Islamic book,' or an 'Islamic course,' or an 'Islamic teacher,' we mean that the religion of Islam permits, condones, and endorses the book, course, or teacher.

If something is described as 'Islamic,' Allah and the Messenger, peace and blessings upon him, would approve of it, making it intrinsically praiseworthy. So when we refer to 'Islamic terrorism,' we're effectively saying that terrorism is permitted, condoned, endorsed, and even praised by Islam. In other words, we're lying.

By definition, there cannot be an 'Islamic sin.' There can be no such thing as 'Islamic theft,' or 'Islamic murder,' or 'Islamic rape,' either, because these things are all sins that are forbidden by Islam. And in exactly the same way, there can be no such thing as 'Islamic terrorism.'

The phrase 'Islamic terrorism' is an attempt to demean the religion of Islam, but in reality, it actually elevates the status of the terrorists. By using the term 'Islamic' to describe them, we're giving them a great honor and a noble status that they don't deserve. They claim faith, but their actions are sinful and antithetical to the ethical, moral, spiritual, and legal teachings of Islam.

So, what should we call them, then? The categorization we read in the Quran is *munafiqun*, or 'hypocrites' – defined as those who spread destruction on Earth while claiming to be believers. The extent to which they harm innocent people is the extent to which they are contradicting the teachings of

Islam, and fulfilling the Quranic description of those whose final abode is Hell.

Islam-hate is real

What's the result of two decades of blasphemously calling terrorism 'Islamic'? Well, in a nutshell, a lot of people hate Islam now. And it's not because of how much we pray. The logic of Islam-opponents is as simple as it is flawed, and terrorists depend on it. It goes something like this: terrorists attack innocent people in the name of Islam. Therefore, there must be something in Islam itself that causes terrorism. In all honesty, if that were true, I'd probably hate Islam too.

The mass media organizations know that they'll get higher ratings and sell more newspapers with headlines and stories that link Islam with terrorism, which reinforces the problem. And to make matters worse, populist politicians realize they can capitalize on the feelings of the masses by offering a solution: ban Islam, in some way, shape, or form. 'We're not racist,' they say. 'We're the only ones doing something about this very serious problem.'

Every time a politician runs for office on a campaign of hate (and especially when he or she wins), the hated community suffers a dramatic increase in violent attacks. Mosques are petrol bombed, or pigs' heads are thrown into them. (May Allah protect the innocent animals from such human cruelty.)

Innocent people are shot and killed, particularly in the USA, where guns are more readily available. Muslim women are attacked on the streets. These things are real, and for every crime reported, many more occur. And for every violent crime, there are many cases of verbal abuse that go unreported.

I once saw a US TV show in which a gun owner explained why he dips his bullets into pigs' blood. He genuinely believed that we Muslims think that being shot and killed by a bullet treated in this way would make *us* go to Hell. When I heard this, I was in stitches!

Spreading peace when others don't

All of this does raise a question though. How are believers supposed to respond in the face of such ignorance and hatred? Are we really expected to continue being peaceful?

In a word, yes. We find that the Path of Peace, as laid out by the Quran and the Prophetic legacy, is precisely that. The more we learn about the Prophet, peace and blessings upon him, the more obvious it becomes. Even in the face of total bigotry, insult, and ignorance we are to respond with peace and loving kindness, just as he did.

Anyone can be peaceful when others are reciprocating, but the spiritual path is to be peaceful, loving, and kind, even in the face of insult. All the prophets with all of their obstacles, and the epic stories of how they handled them, are examples for us. They showed us how to be graceful in the face of ignorance.

The Quran makes it crystal clear how we are to respond when confronted by the ignorant:

> 'And the servants of the Most Loving are those who walk on the Earth in humility, and when the ignorant address them, they say, "Peace!"'[4]

Responding peacefully from the Inside-Out

I never understood how it was possible that Allah, the Source of Love and Peace, demanded such great forbearance from us. That is, until I realized the Inside-Out nature of life. Because we're always *feeling our own thinking*, not the insults of another person, of course it makes sense that we're capable of not letting our own hurt feelings stop us from treating others with respect.

A person's insults literally cannot hurt us – only *the way we think about* their words can hurt us. When someone insults you, it's as if they offer you a cup of poison. When you take it to heart, you drink the poison. The fact that you can choose whether or not to take it to heart means that it's not the insult itself, but *the way you think about the insult*, that does the damage.

On one occasion the Prophet, peace and blessings upon him, was sitting with his best friend, Abu Bakr, may Allah be pleased with him. Abu Bakr was renowned for being a very peace-loving, gentle man. However, someone who hated Islam came over to them and started hurling insults at Abu Bakr. The Prophet, peace and blessings upon him, stayed seated, smiled, and silently watched with curiosity. After taking the abuse quietly, Abu Bakr finally responded to the comments. The Prophet, peace and blessings upon him, immediately showed his disapproval, got up and left.

Abu Bakr must have been so confused at this point. His best friend had not only failed to defend him, he'd also smiled as he was being insulted and then walked off when he started defending himself! At the same time, he must have known that his friend was an enlightened man, and a prophet sent from Allah. So he probably knew that his beloved friend must have been *thinking* about things somewhat differently from him.

When Abu Bakr caught up with the Prophet Muhammad, peace and blessings upon him, he said to him, 'O Messenger of Allah, he was abusing me and you remained sitting. When I responded to him, you disapproved and got up.'

The Prophet explained that when Abu Bakr was sitting peacefully, in silence, an angel had been with him, responding on his behalf. However, as soon as he started reacting to the abuse, the angel left, and Satan took its place. So the Prophet also left. The Prophet, peace and blessings upon him, then said:

> *'If a person is wronged and he forbears it just for the sake of Allah the Almighty, Allah will honor him and give him the upper hand with His help.'*[5]

Being a true Muslim

This is what it means to be a true Muslim; a true source of peace for humanity, and a true follower of the Prophet, peace and blessings upon him. Here are some words of wisdom from an early scholar and spiritual master of the Islamic tradition, describing a true Muslim:

'The true Muslim is like the Earth.
All filthy and disgusting things are cast upon it,
But only beautiful things grow from it.'

Imam Junayd

To be a true Muslim, then, in an age when Islam is the most hated religion in the world, means that we say about those who hate us:

- They can hate us. But they can never stop us from loving them.
- They can lie and slander our religion. But we'll only speak the truth to them.
- They can fear us. But we'll always be there for them, ready to protect them.
- They can mock and ridicule us. But we'll only do good to them.

- They can look down on us. But we'll always see them as equals and never look up to them.
- They can join us. But we'll never join them.

Because in the end, these people were never our teachers. The Prophet Muhammad, peace and blessings upon him, is our teacher. And what he taught us is the noble path of all of the prophets of Allah. So whatever the Opponents of Peace do or say, we won't fall off this path, just because of them.

CHAPTER 8

Presence – the Key to Paradise

'Can the reward for Spiritual Excellence
be anything other than Spiritual Excellence?'[1]

QURAN

The Prophet Muhammad, peace and blessings upon him, said:

'Ihsan *[Spiritual Excellence] is to worship Allah as if you see Him; and though you cannot, know that He sees you.'*[2]

This saying of the Prophet, peace and blessings upon him, appeared in Chapter 1 of this book, where I shared the longer version, known as the *hadith* of Gabriel. Along with the whole Quran, this Prophetic saying is the starting point of the entire spiritual tradition within Islam. If it weren't for this inner spiritual dimension, the religion would become dry and stale for a believer, because our actions would not be infused with an awareness of the presence of Allah, the Ever-Present.

In this chapter, I share the personal insights I've had about this Prophetic saying; these have brought immense benefit to my life, and to the lives of my students. I also reveal how the Inside-Out Paradigm, by Allah's grace, has enabled me to live a more spiritually excellent, fully present life.

In the above saying, the Arabic word I'm translating as 'Spiritual Excellence' is *Ihsan.* All of the descriptions of *Ihsan* that I've read seem to suggest that there are two main dimensions to it: being present, and doing actions that are more than just 'good.' An essential requirement for *Ihsan* is presence infused into the actions we're doing. There may be more to it that I've not yet seen, but presence is most certainly a prerequisite for *Ihsan*, and its most essential component.

What is presence?

When I realized this, the Prophetic saying that defines the state of *Ihsan* took on a much more significant meaning in my life. It became clear to me that this short statement of the Prophet, peace and blessings upon him, contains within it the three main ways that we can all instantly become 'present.'

Before I share them with you, let me explain what I mean by 'presence.' To be present is to have your full awareness and attention in *this* moment – not in the future or the past. In reality, only this moment actually exists. The future, in this moment, is only a thought-generated imagination of what may or may not happen. The past, in this moment, is only a memory, which is also thought. In reality, there is only now.

This is an essential spiritual concept because we can only be with Allah now, in this moment. We can only devote ourselves to Allah now, in this moment. We can only have insight now, in this moment. Our only responsibility now, is to be aware of Allah's presence – now, not tomorrow or yesterday. Not even later today, but *right now*. Without a deep awareness of this present moment, our minds are preoccupied with fantasies, and we lose track of reality.

The three ways to become present

The secrets of how to become present are embedded within one saying of the Prophet, peace and blessings upon him. I'll share the teaching and my reflections on it.

1. 'Worship Allah'

'*Ihsan* (Spiritual Excellence/Presence) is to *worship Allah* as if you see Him; and though you cannot, know that He sees you.'

Before we explore the first secret, I want to make a quick point about 'worship.' To worship Allah means to devote ourselves to Allah, which is often done through formulae of worship like praying and fasting.

However, it's important to know that anything – from reading a book to physical exercise, from working to playing, and from eating to making love – can be considered worship when it's done from a place of sincere devotion to Allah. Unlike in some other religious traditions, sex is considered praiseworthy in Islam and is rewarded when it's done with the right intention. A Muslim's aim in life is not just to pray five times a day, but to make his or her whole life a prayer.

So, how does 'worshipping Allah' make us more present? Prayer is a good metaphor for life. By learning to pray well, we learn to live well. The secret to prayer lies in this fact: we can't worship Allah in the past or the future. If we 'worship' Allah through acts of devotion with a mind that isn't present, we're not *really* worshipping Allah – we're just going through the motions of it.

This is why the Prophet, peace and blessings upon him, said:

> *'Someone will pray and only half of their prayer will be accepted, or a quarter, or an eighth, or a sixteenth, or less than that.'*[3]

The key to having more of the prayer accepted lies in how present the worshipper is while they pray. Subtly embedded within this command is the first secret to presence: 'Worship Allah.' This is a direct command, and in order to follow it, we're required to pour our full attention into what we're doing. And this is the secret: when you pour all of your attention, or energy, or 'self,' into any action, you're automatically present.

The power of attention

You can try this for yourself, right now. Put all of your attention into what you're doing. Right now, you're reading this book. Are you fully here? Or is your mind wandering? Pour all of yourself into reading this book, just as all of my attention is here, as I write. By doing so, the act of reading is infused with presence. In other words, by being present as you read, you're reading with Spiritual Excellence, with *Ihsan*.

This isn't limited to reading, writing, prayer, and other forms of worship. It applies to literally everything in life. Wherever you are, whatever you're doing, do it with all of yourself. This is the Prophetic Way – perhaps one of the most beneficial Prophetic examples that we can start living.

If we're unaware of the importance of 'presence of heart,' when we see an intensely present person and notice that there's something special about them, we'll have no idea what it *is* that makes them special. What makes them special is their spiritual presence. Inculcating spiritual presence is the essence of worship and what's known as *dhikr*, or remembrance of Allah. (You'll learn more about *dhikr* in Chapter 8.)

In the Quran, Allah says:

> 'Indeed, whoever turns his face to Allah, and is spiritually excellent,
> for him is a reward from his Lord,
> and there is no fear for him, nor shall he grieve.'[4]

The Quran sometimes uses the Arabic expression 'turning your face toward Allah.' This doesn't just mean your physical face – it means 'your essence,' or 'all of yourself.' Anything done by pouring all of your energy into it, or with your full present awareness, makes you 'spiritually excellent,' and the activity becomes a form of prayer. The only thing required is your full attention.

When you're walking down the street, you can do so just to get where you're going, or you can walk knowing that with each footstep, you've already arrived home: into Allah's presence. When you're eating, you can eat to finish the food, or you can eat while being fully aware of, and enjoying, every mouthful of delicious, nourishing sustenance.

When you're working, you can work to complete the project, or you can pour your full attention into the part of the project you're working on right now. In doing so, you'll likely complete the project faster, with more ease, and with less unnecessary thinking.

An action done with Spiritual Excellence is an action done with beauty and elegance. This is how the '*baraka*,' or 'spiritual blessing,' of actions is manifest. In other words, this is how you get in 'the zone' or 'the flow.'

2. 'As if you see Him, though you cannot'

'*Ihsan* (Spiritual Excellence/Presence) is to worship Allah *as if you see Him; and though you cannot,* know that He sees you.'

It's interesting that the Prophet, peace and blessings upon him, says 'as if you see Him,' when he knows that this is impossible. (As I explained earlier, Allah is beyond gender, and the pronoun 'Him' is used for convenience.) Any thought you have of Allah, is not Allah, by definition. Allah is unimaginable, by definition.

During my seminars, I sometimes ask audience members to 'imagine Allah,' and tell me what they see. At first they are confused, so I persist, saying: 'When you're in prayer, and you're engaged in the act of prayer, trying to concentrate, what do you see when you think about Allah?'

The answers people give always fascinate me – they range from a 'white light' to the Kaba in Mecca, from Heaven to Hell, and many other things; children sometimes give hilarious answers. Regardless of the response, I point out that whatever we were imagining during prayer, is not Allah. So if we were worshipping that image, we were, in a subtle way, associating something that is not Allah, with Allah. The Quran says in this respect:

> 'Say: Allah is One. Allah is eternal. He begot no one nor was He begotten. Nothing is comparable to Him.'[5]

The fact that nothing is comparable to Him means, as a wise man once said, 'Whatever you think Allah is, that is not Allah.'

This is what I'm getting at: we can't imagine or 'see' Allah. This is the second secret to presence: the closest we can ever be to 'seeing' Allah, is to free our minds altogether from thoughts. To be present: to have 'presence of heart,' as the great twelfth-century Persian theologian and mystic Imam Abu Hamid al-Ghazali, may Allah be pleased with him, called it. So, let's explore how to do that.

Notice the gap between thoughts

You may have noticed that your thinking can go very 'fast,' and that you can be engaged in a 'stream of consciousness' in which one thought leads to another, and another. During prayer we might engage in a train of thinking that goes like this:

Allah… Heaven. Oh, I want to go there; maybe I will if I can just sin less… Oh dear, it's too bad that I insulted my father the other day. I know that's a big sin. But then, he was being so stubborn… Oh, that reminds me: I must speak to that stubborn guy at work tomorrow and make sure he hands in the report… Oh, I wonder if my friend's back from holiday yet… Boy, I could do with a holiday… As-Salam Alaikum… *wait, the prayer's already over?!*

Before long, the whole prayer can be lost in random, imaginary thinking that may have started with Allah, or something holy, but quickly descended into the mundane things of this world that have nothing to do with what we're actually saying or doing in the prayer. When this happens, it's common that a prayer ends and we realize that we're not even aware of which sections of the Quran we've just recited.

Just as thinking can appear to go very fast, it can also slow down. You can even slow down enough to notice that there's a 'gap' between one thought and the next. When you put your attention into the gap, it's as if you're 'thinking about' nothing. It seems as if your thinking has stopped, if only for a few seconds.

This is the state of presence, from which real prayer can happen. You don't need to do this all the time – you just need to know that entering this state is possible, and that you can enter it relatively easily.

Here's something that may allow you to have an experience of this state, right now. I'm going to ask you a question. I want you to read it, ponder it, and pause before reading on. Ready? Okay, I want you to ask yourself:

I wonder what my next thought will be… and then pause.

Now that you've continued reading, I want you to do it again, for a little longer, and see if you can do so without jumping to any conclusions:

I wonder what my next thought will be… and then pause.

As you did this, you may have noticed that a few seconds elapsed without a new thought. Perhaps you quietened your mind and entered a state of awareness – of 'no-mind' – without fully engaging in any particular thought. *That* is presence. To worship Allah 'as if you see Him,' is to notice the gap of pure consciousness that exists in between thoughts.

3. *'Know that He sees you'*

'*Ihsan* (Spiritual Excellence/Presence) is to worship Allah as if you see Him; and though you cannot, *know that He sees you*.'

The third way you can become present right now is to be aware that Allah, the Infinite Intelligence Behind Life, sees you, and is with you right now. Take a moment to become consciously aware of this, now. Allah is watching you. You may even notice that the angels are with you and watching you, if you're aware of their existence. Do this now.

As you become aware that Allah is watching you, I have a question for you: 'Where did your attention go?' You may like to try this again, right now. Realize that Allah is watching you as you read this. Now notice where your attention goes as you become aware that Allah is watching you.

Most people notice that their attention goes within. When I do this, I become much more aware of my body: I notice how I'm sitting. Allah, the Master of the Universe, is watching me – what am I doing with myself?

This is the third way of instantly becoming present: putting your attention into your body. Notice how you're sitting. Notice how it feels to sit that way. Notice how it feels to be inside your own skin, right now. It may be an intense feeling – if you're going through a lot – or it may be hardly noticeable… until you notice it.

The 'Inner Salam Method'

By putting part of your attention into your body as you do an action, you automatically become more present. Just by noticing that Allah is with you, and hence, by noticing your physical self, you become present, and free from thoughts about the past and the future.

Anxiety is largely based on thoughts about the future. Depression is usually based on thoughts about the past. To be present is to free yourself from both of these traps of the ego. We can think about the past and the future in delightful ways too, but this is still not reality. Reality is what exists now, in this moment. By putting your full attention into your body when you're feeling bad, without getting caught up with the thoughts in your mind, you can notice your intense feelings pass, in the presence of your full awareness.

I call this the 'Inner *Salam* Method' because the feelings inevitably pass and are replaced with a sense of inner peace (*salam*). This is particularly useful when we're too upset to think straight, or to listen sensibly to any advice given that might benefit us. All upsets seem to dissolve in the energy of our presence.

A final point about this Prophetic saying of *Ihsan*, and its relationship to presence, is offered by Shaykh Dr. Abdalqadir as-Sufi, the great scholar and spiritual master. In a discourse on the topic of love, he noted that the Quran states that Allah loves those who are 'spiritually excellent.' He then explained this Prophetic saying and, in doing so, noted that to be aware that Allah is watching us requires us to shift from being the 'observer' to the 'observed.'

It moves us from being the 'subject' or 'doer' of our own lives, to being the 'object' of life – being observed by the true Subject of life: Allah. Suddenly, Allah becomes the Subject, and we're merely the objects being observed. *This* is reality.

Summary of the three ways to be present

- **Worship Allah** – pour all of your attention into what you're doing.
- **As though you see Him, though you cannot** – clear your mind by noticing the 'gap' between thoughts.
- **Know that He sees you** – notice that you're being observed, and in doing so, notice what's happening now, in your body.

The value of a clear mind

For a believing Muslim, one of the greatest and immediately noticeable benefits to bringing the light of presence to our life is how dramatically it enhances our experience of prayer. We're so blessed to have five opportunities built into every day where we can deliberately enter a state of presence and absorb the depth of the Quran, which is recited in the prayer.

Presence is a requisite for insight. By being consciously aware during our prayers, we're in the psychological and spiritual state that makes us fertile for life-enhancing insight to occur. In a sacred saying, the Prophet, peace and blessings upon him, told us that Allah says:

> *'My servant does not draw near to Me with anything more loved by Me than what I have made obligatory. My servant continues to draw nearer to Me with additional devotions until I love him.*
>
> *'When I love him, I become the hearing with which he hears, the sight with which he sees, the hand with which he works, and the foot with which he walks. Were he to ask for something, I would surely give it, and were he to ask for refuge, I would surely grant him refuge.'*[6]

This is one of my personal favorite sayings of the Prophet, peace and blessings upon him. As we engage more fully with presence of heart, in prayer and *dhikr* (remembrance of Allah), this statement takes on more meaning, and makes more sense.

By being fully present, you begin to realize something profound: although your eyes cannot see Allah, Allah sees through your eyes. As we gain more appreciation for this state of *Ihsan*, and deliberately enter it more often, we begin to realize how valuable it is. We're more effective, more aware, and feel closer to Allah when we're present.

Effortless presence from the Inside-Out

For me, one of the greatest gifts of insightfully realizing the Inside-Out Reality was suddenly finding myself in a much deeper state of presence during prayer, without trying to be. The Inside-Out took an enormous amount of unnecessary thinking off my mind. It was as if the subtle logic of the paradigm kept giving me surprising, unexpected gifts.

But why did understanding the Inside-Out give me a much more clear and present mind? When we believe, mistakenly, that a situation not turning out the way we want will make us feel really bad, or that a situation turning out exactly the way we want will make us feel really good, it's almost impossible not to think about that situation! Our energy and attention is taken away from what's real – the moment – and into what's imaginary: how we think we'll feel when a particular future event occurs.

However, when we're fully aware that no future, current, or past event can possibly cause our feelings, we're much less inclined to think about those events. It's really hard to be preoccupied with something that you know is impossible – it's *literally impossible* that anything other than thought can cause feelings.

In other words, transcending the Outside-In Illusion leaves us with much less on our minds. And the less we have on our minds, the more present we are. The more present we are, the more aware we are of the divine presence.

'If you want eternal paradise, fully immerse yourself into this moment.'

Elif Shifak

CHAPTER 9

Remembrance – the Spiritual Cure

'Everything that is in the heavens and the Earth is exalting Allah, the Sovereign, the Pure, the Almighty, the Wise.'[1]

QURAN

Everything in the Universe, from the smallest particle to the largest star, is worshipping and praising Allah – by doing exactly what Allah commands it to do. This is true for every living being, except the one who uses his or her free will to ignore the existence of the divine.

Dhikr: remembrance of Allah

Every quark of every atom, of every molecule, of every cell, of every tissue, of every organ system in your body is worshipping Allah by doing precisely what Allah wills. However, insofar as we're forgetful of Allah's presence, we're rebelling against this divine order. The moment we turn inward, and become aware of our true selves and the infinite divine presence, we return to balance and harmony with the cosmos. This is *dhikr.*

Pronounced 'thi-kr,' *dhikr* is the Arabic word for 'remembrance,' or to bring something to mind. The moment we do this, there's a powerful, sublime effect – a deep feeling of gratitude and reverence that overtakes the heart. Allah, the Transcendent, says in the Quran:

> 'Remember Me, and I will remember you.'[2]

In a beautiful saying, the Prophet, peace and blessings upon him, said that Allah, the Most High, says:

> *'I am according to the opinion that my servant has of Me. I am with him whenever he remembers me. If he remembers Me in his heart, I remember him in my "heart"; if he remembers Me in a gathering, I remember him in a greater gathering; if he draws near to me by a hand's span, I draw near to him an arm's length; if he draws near to me an arm's length, I draw near to him by several feet; and if he comes to me walking, I go to him running.'*[3]

The Prophet, peace and blessings upon him, also said:

> *'The difference between someone who remembers their Lord and someone who does not, is like the difference between the living and the dead.'*[4]

Spiritual life and depth is inculcated in our hearts through 'remembrance.' This is what makes our hearts stronger and softer. This is what allows us to become more alive, spiritually.

In another simple statement, the Prophet, peace and blessings upon him, summarized the essence of Islam in a few words:

> *'Keep Allah in mind wherever you are; follow a wrong with a right that offsets it; and treat people courteously.'*[5]

Understanding *dhikr*

In a spiritual context, the Quran often refers to '*dhikr Allah*,' the remembrance of Allah's infinite presence. By becoming aware of the present moment, we're free from everything that might distract us from *dhikr*.

By letting go of unnecessary thinking, we spend more time in the present moment – the only space within which true *dhikr* is possible. We can only be at one with the Infinite in the present. It could be said that presence is the psychological state of *dhikr Allah*.

In a beautiful poem called *Purification of the Heart*, written by a Mauritanian scholar, the 24 'diseases of the spiritual heart' are outlined and, one by one, a cure is given for each. In 2004, Shaykh Hamza Yusuf, one of the leaders of Muslims in the West, translated the poem for us, and added some commentary in English. Knowledge of this text, or a similar one that covers this subject matter, is considered obligatory for every individual Muslim to know.

Some of these diseases, and the ways in which to transcend them, are covered in Chapter 16, based on an understanding of the Inside-Out Paradigm. After careful consideration, we can see that every one of the spiritual diseases is based on the Outside-In Illusion that our feelings might be coming from somewhere other than Allah, through some mechanism other than thought.

One of the most remarkable things about the poem, aside from its depth and eloquence, is that each of the cures given involve remembering Allah (*dhikr*) in one form or another. And the overall cure given for all of the diseases of the heart is expounded at the end of the poem. This essential cure is found in the following Quran verse:

> 'Is it not through the remembrance of Allah that the hearts attain tranquility?'[6]

Remembering Allah abundantly

Many spiritual people are familiar with the idea of a 'mantra': a practice that's prevalent in Hindu and Buddhist traditions. The etymology of the word is fascinating. In Sanskrit, 'man' means 'mind,' and 'tra' means 'tool.' A mantra is a formula that's repeated over and over again, as a tool, designed to free the mind. This is very similar to the Muslim *dhikr*.

Dhikr involves bringing Allah to mind through the act of deliberately mentioning Allah with our tongue. This is highly recommended by the Quran in several verses:

> 'Dear Believers, Remember Allah often and with a lot of remembrance, and glorify
> Him in the morning and evening.'[7]

> 'And men who remember Allah much,
> and women who remember Allah much,
> Allah has prepared for them forgiveness
> and a vast reward.'[8]

In fact, Allah even says in the Quran:

> 'And the remembrance of Allah is the greatest deed, without doubt.'[9]

By bringing the Infinite Source of all experience to our minds, we're freed from the petty, illusory concerns of the things of this world, which we falsely imagine are the source of our feelings. Again, it's not the *things* of this world that are the problem. The problem is that we imagine that those *things* can cause our felt experience of life. *Dhikr* is a constant remembrance of the true source of our experience.

In fact, we could think of the whole Quran as a 600-page 'mantra.' The Quran says that it is, itself, a most powerful form of remembrance:

'It [the Quran] is a remembrance [dhikr] for all the worlds.'[10]

The Prophet, peace and blessings upon him, confirmed this by saying:

*'The Quran is the Clarifying Light, the Wise Remembrance [*dhikr*], and the Straight Path.'*[11]

The healing power of dhikr

The belief that bringing Allah to mind can cure our psychological suffering is not merely superstition. There's a very particular mechanism through which it works. Below, I've demonstrated precisely how 'remembrance' can have such a healing effect and relieve us from our psychological suffering. Given that *true* remembrance of Allah has the power to cure our psycho-spiritual ailments, it's no wonder that Muslims are encouraged to make it a part of their daily lives.

The Quran verse above refers precisely to the psychological cure that humanity has been searching for: remembrance of Allah. But to understand how it works, we must understand the Inside-Out Paradigm. This 'remembrance of Allah' is then made immediately relevant to us, and personally impactful, and doesn't require faith in any particular religion. The Quran was, after all, sent to benefit all of humanity, not just Muslims.

The three types of **dhikr**

Before we explore how this psychological and spiritual cure-all works, let's take a look at the three main categories of *dhikr*.

Remembrance of the tongue

This can take many forms, including Quran recitation and continuously repeating short phrases mentioning Allah.

Remembrance of the heart

This involves being deeply aware of Allah's infinite presence in our hearts. The moment we're dragged away from the present moment, due to Outside-In thinking, we're no longer remembering Allah with our hearts.

Remembrance of the heart and the tongue.

This is the optimal way of performing *dhikr*, from which all of the benefits of the practice are manifest. This is the aim of all those who do *dhikr*. Some people become so immensely aware of the present moment, and of Allah's presence, that they can't help but thank and praise Allah. Others find that by deliberately remembering Allah with the tongue, habitually, they're reminded of the presence of Allah more often, and so are more inclined to be aware of Allah's presence.

Psychological *dhikr* from the Inside-Out

Remembering Allah from the 'Outside-In' – the illusion that something other than Allah, via thought in the moment, can cause feelings – is to not *truly* remember Allah. In other words, it's a remembrance that can only occur on the tongue. It can't penetrate to the heart, due to a misunderstanding on the part of the devotee.

If we're convinced that our felt experience of life is coming from somewhere other than Allah via thought, we can try to help ourselves with verbal utterances. But in our hearts and minds, we're not really aware of Allah's role in creating our current-moment felt experience. A beautiful and commonly known Quranic and Prophetic formula of *dhikr* is: 'There is no might or power except Allah.'

In psychological terms, there is no might or power that can cause our feelings, except Allah, through thought. But do you see how someone could repeat this phrase over and over without realizing this distinction? In so doing, they're saying that Allah is the source of all power, without being aware that only Allah – not the situation – is the source of their feelings.

For me as a Muslim, one of the most relevant and powerful dimensions of the Inside-Out Paradigm is the fact that it gives us an understanding that allows us to experience real, *psychological dhikr*. This *dhikr* is not a formula, but an impactful, relevant, insightful 'remembering' of the role of Allah in creating our experience, which frees us from the spiritual and psychological traps of the ego.

All of our psychological suffering comes from putting our feelings onto objects. If we can see the objects without the feelings, we're psychologically healthy. When we see that Allah is the true source of our feelings, we automatically see the objects without the feelings we were attaching to them. In this way, *dhikr* makes us psychologically healthy. In other words, when we realize that thought – not the object we're thinking about – is the source of our feelings, we realign ourselves with reality.

This is the simple, comprehensive psychological cure humanity has always been searching for. This truth is contained in every spiritual tradition, and Sydney Banks, may he rest in peace, gave us the psychological terms through which we can understand it.

When a Muslim is present, and aligned with the Inside-Out Reality, he or she almost can't help but fill his/her tongue with abundant gratitude and praise of Allah. He or she becomes among those who remember Allah in their hearts, and their tongues and bodies respond with praise. They're thus realigned with the beautiful divine order of the rest of existence.

Dhikr in daily life

From the moment I wake up, I'm engaged in *dhikr*, in precisely the way recommended by the Prophet, peace and blessings upon him. When my eyes open, the first thought and words I utter are: 'All gratitude and praise is due to Allah, who gave us life after death and to whom we will return.'

I then go to the bathroom, and before entering it I say: 'Allah, I seek refuge in You from dirt and filth.' I wash myself in the exact way the Prophet, peace and blessings upon him, taught us, starting with these words: 'In the name of Allah, the Most Loving, the Most Kind.' The use of water in the morning becomes a spiritual act of remembering the divine.

Next, I either walk to the mosque, or I go to the part of my home used for prayer. I then engage in the pre-dawn *Fajr* prayer, grateful for the mere fact that I'm alive for another day. I'm grateful to have been blessed with this prayer of gratitude.

After prayer, I recite the Quran. Upon leaving the house Muslims say: 'Allah, I take refuge with You, lest I should stray or be led astray, or slip or be tripped, or oppress or be oppressed, behave foolishly or be treated foolishly.'

The Prophet, peace and blessings upon him, gave us dozens of prayers that can be infused into all of our daily actions, from washing to leaving the house, and from putting on our clothes to eating and working, and everything in between. These prayers have many purposes. The first, and most important, is that they remind us, habitually, to be present and mindful of Allah, thereby fulfilling the inner purpose of our existence.

When I'm traveling, I always have my favorite music playlist loaded up on my cell phone, ready to listen to. I play my favorite songs over and over, as I travel from one place to another. I know about the importance of presence, so I'll sometimes deliberately be present and aware of Allah's presence as I do this. I find that around 80 percent of the time, I'll fall into thinking about an imagined future or a remembered past. The other 20 percent of the time, I'm able to be intently present.

Occasionally, for some reason or another, the music on my phone isn't available, so I'll sit quietly on the train, or walk without anything in my ears. I soon find myself, almost without trying or thinking about it, being present and filling my tongue and heart with remembrance of Allah. I recite all the Quran I know from memory, or repeat formulae such as:

- '*Alhamdulillah* – all gratitude and praise is due to Allah.'
- '*Subhan Allah* – Allah is Transcendent.'
- '*Allah Akbar* – Allah is the Greatest.'
- '*La ilaha il-Allah* – there is no God, except Allah.'

I soon realized that when I'm doing this, I'm present for around 80 percent of the time, and absent-minded – thinking about the past or future – for much less of the time. All of the Quran that I've memorized comes to life, and is on the tip of my tongue, with no risk of it being lost.

My heart soon fills up with awe, gratitude, and love for Allah and all of humanity and creation. I look at people, read their faces, then send them loving, uplifting energy, or I use words to pray for them in my mind. All of a sudden, the entire trip becomes a deep inward journey into the Soul of Life, and I arrive at my destination before I know it.

Because of this profound shift in the quality of my life, it made sense for me to listen to music much less often, and instead to engage in these forms of *dhikr* for most or all of my journeys. Most of the time I'm using public transportation I'll do this. That is, of course, with one, somewhat bizarre, exception.

Flying while Muslim

If there's ever a time when you really want there to be a religious, spiritual person praying near you, it's while you're sat in a tin can floating some 35,000 feet above the ground. And if there's one thing I want to be doing when I'm in that tin can, it's reciting the Quran. And yet I refrain from doing so, especially if I'm in the USA, because I know that someone on the plane is likely to become afraid and report me as suspicious.

This is so unfortunate, yet it happens for obvious reasons. The collective consciousness of the West has been scarred by the events of 9/11 and their aftermath, and a Muslim aboard a plane just doesn't seem like a good fit. Unless, of course, you know what Islam is and what Muslims believe in. All the fear and suspicion around Islam doesn't make us any safer, it just makes us… well, afraid and suspicious.

One of the worst ideas people have about Islam is that the more religious an individual is, the more likely he or she is to become a terrorist. This is completely untrue and there's absolutely no evidence for it. Most terrorists have no connection with their faith and are irreligious – until they become radicalized, which, according to some studies, takes as little as 3–6 months. The 9/11 terrorists went to strip clubs before doing the attacks.

In fact, having a well-established religious identity protects against violent radicalization. This should all just be common sense, though. We really don't need to worry about people worshipping *more.*[12]

However, because of this persistent myth, a Muslim man was removed from a plane for saying the words *insha'Allah*, which mean 'God willing.' Another was removed because his name made the stewardess suspicious of him – to be fair, it was 'Mohamed Ahmed.' This name literally means 'the one worthy of praise and gratitude' and 'the one who is grateful and praiseful.'

I travel to California several times a year to lead workshops and training for professional coaches looking to grow their businesses, and if there's one thing I've noticed during all those trips, it's that *every single* time I fly to the USA, I'm randomly selected for extra security checks. If there are a dozen people ahead of me and behind me, I'm still always 'randomly' selected.

My hope and prayer is that soon in the West there will be a deeper, genuine understanding of what Islam is, and what it's not. I hope that one day, when people see a religious Muslim on a plane, they'll be delighted and actually feel safer, knowing that someone near them will be praying for them.

I hope that one day, people won't look down on Muslims as potential criminals but look up to them as sources of spiritual guidance. I hope that one day, people realize that a believing Muslim is a light for humanity who can't harm anyone intentionally – by definition – and is not someone to be feared, but instead, honored.

'There are some people who are the keys to Allah's remembrance. When they are seen, Allah is remembered.'[13]

The Prophet Muhammad, peace and blessings upon him

CHAPTER 10

Speaking Truth – the Highest Form of Courage

'Dear Believers, be aware of Allah and
be upright in your speech –
He will straighten out your affairs and
forgive your sins for you.'[1]

QURAN

When you remember Allah, you're better at speaking the truth. Truth in its absolute form, '*al-Haqq*,' is one of Allah's 99 names in Islam. The great Indian leader Mahatma Gandhi once said, 'I worship the same God as the Muslims – that is, Truth.'

For a spiritual seeker, Truth is the aim. When we hear it, it resonates with our souls. As much as it's a delight for us to hear words of truth, it's harmful for us to speak anything other than truth.

In the Islamic spiritual tradition, there are 20 destructive qualities of the tongue and only one praiseworthy quality: 'speaking truth.' Speaking the truth is one of the most highly emphasized 'good actions' in Islam. The most direct and powerful way for us to improve our character, and increase our personal ethical and spiritual awareness, is to be deliberately impeccable with the power of our word.

To emphasize this fact, here are some teachings of our beloved Prophet, peace and blessings upon him, who we believe is the best of humanity, in action and speech:

'May God have mercy on a servant
who has spoken well and gained good,
or kept silent and avoided harm.'[2]

'The characteristics of a hypocrite are three:
When he speaks, he lies;
When he gives his word, he breaks it;
When he is given a trust, he is unfaithful.'[3]

'The servants Allah loves most,
are those who are most sincere with Allah's servants.'[4]

Instead of trying to use willpower to force ourselves to be more truthful, we can insightfully be transformed by exploring these questions: 'What is it that prevents us from being truthful?' 'Why is it that we're sometimes deceitful, or avoid speaking truthfully and kindly to people?'

The Psychology of Deceit

There are two main reasons we lie and insult others: because we fear harm and because we desire benefit, both natural human inclinations. The mistake is to believe that lying or insulting others will get us there. This mistake is rooted in the psychological Outside-In Illusion, but this isn't obvious until we explore it in more depth.

All of our fears are fears of feelings: we think that if things don't turn out the way we want them to, we'll feel bad. All of our desires are also desires of feelings: we think that if things *do* turn out the way we want them to, we'll feel good. The truth is that feelings can't come from anything other than Allah, via thought in the moment. So, what do we really desire? And what are we really afraid of?

The most wonderful feeling in the world can only come from thought in the moment. And the worst feeling imaginable can also only come from within. We live our whole lives so afraid of feeling bad, or trying to feel good, that this obvious fact escapes our attention.

We spend our whole lives doing anything and everything necessary to fix and change the outside world – all to gain for ourselves something that can come only from within. Part of this attempt to control the outside world in a futile attempt to feel better, involves lying to those we love, or not having the courage to tell them the truth. As the Prophet, peace and blessings upon him, said:

'Speak truth, even though it be bitter.'[5]

Courage from the Inside-Out

In Islam, speaking the truth to someone more powerful than you is considered the highest form of courage. In the story of Moses, peace and blessings upon him, the prophet was told by Allah to go to the Pharaoh of Egypt, the biggest, most terrifying tyrant on the face of the Earth at that time, who had been killing the first-born males in each family because of a dream he'd had. The pharaoh was persecuting the Jews, and of course he had it in for Moses. And yet the Quran says that Allah said to Moses:

> 'And speak to him [the Pharaoh] with gentle words, so that perhaps he may be reminded...'[6]

How was Moses, peace and blessings upon him, expected to be courageous enough to speak with this terrifyingly powerful dictator using *gentle* words?! Knowing the Inside-Out, this becomes easier to understand: a tyrant literally doesn't have the ability to *cause* fear inside anyone. There's no doubt he could harm us physically, but fearing that harm in advance is something that we do in our own minds.

All feelings, and all experience – including fear – can only come from Allah, and only through fearful thinking in the moment. When we realize this, we automatically have the courage to do what's required of us. This was exemplified by the Prophet Moses, peace and blessings upon him.

A courageous conversation

Thankfully, I've never had to confront a tyrant. However, for a long while, I was fearful of having a particular conversation with my father. I was talking with a girl and my guess was that my father wouldn't approve of her. Let's just say that what I wanted in a spouse, and what he wanted for me, didn't exactly match up.

For context, my father is a lovely man; he has a very witty sense of humor and is fun to hang out with… unless you happen to be his son. While we were growing up, my siblings and I lived in fear of speaking out and were always prepared to be 'shot down.'

The girl in question was a wonderful young lady from an amazingly loving family – may Allah continue to bless her and her family with divine love, mercy, and guidance. In my family, however, only one person knew about her – my sister, Sonia. She was very happy for me, and reassured me, saying: 'No matter what the rest of our family say, you should be with whoever makes you happy. I just want you to be free and happy. Because I love you.'

It was a really sweet and meaningful thing to hear, especially from someone who didn't talk much about feelings, or give advice. But at the time I was quite shy, embarrassed, and dismissive. *Of course I'll do what I want*, I thought. *I know how to handle the family…*' But my sister knew what she was saying. And little did I know at the time that this beautiful advice would be the last real conversation we'd ever have.

Fast-forward a few months, and I was a grown man who was afraid of breaking the news to my mum, and especially my dad, that I'd found someone. This fear was, of course, completely irrational. Most of our fears are. But I must have been missing something because for a few months before I told my parents, I was dreading it and felt anxious and afraid.

I was trying to do energy healing techniques to release the feeling, but it didn't work. Then it dawned on me: I should put this Inside-Out stuff to the test. So I spoke with my mentor, Dr. Keith Blevens. After he deeply listened to everything that was on my mind, I eventually said to him, 'I know that my feelings come from thought, but in reality, I'm still really afraid of having this conversation with my dad.'

Keith replied: 'Mamoon, there's no way you could possibly know that your feelings of fear are coming from fearful thinking and not from the conversation you're afraid of having.' I knew he was right, but I still didn't get it. Keith continued:

'If you knew your fear was just coming from the way you're thinking, you wouldn't really be afraid any more. You can't really be afraid of something that you know you're creating. No one is ever really afraid of something they know they're creating.

'If you are afraid of it, you clearly don't know that it's your own thinking that's causing your fearful feeling. That would be like drawing a picture of a scary monster, then running out of the room screaming because of the scary monster you'd just drawn.'

The moment he said that, I burst out laughing and suddenly, insightfully, I saw the truth of the Inside-Out Paradigm – yet again. From that point on, I was totally cool about talking to my parents and letting them know what was going on with me.

I genuinely knew that my fear was just thought, and that I didn't need to be concerned about it because the feeling had literally *nothing* to do with the relationship, or my parents, or the conversation I was concerned about having. I knew it was just coming from thought in that moment, which would pass effortlessly, as it always does.

When I did speak with my parents, at first they were surprisingly supportive. And although in the end that relationship didn't work out, I now know that I'm able to speak to my parents, even when I'm pretty certain they won't agree with where I stand. I never needed positive thinking techniques – I just needed to know what can and can't cause feelings.

The sin of backbiting

After very careful research of the subject, the quote below is the closest reference I've found in the Quran to zombies[7]:

> 'Dear Believers... do not backbite one another.
> Would one of you like to eat the flesh of his dead brother?
> You would hate it. So be mindful of Allah.
> Verily, Allah accepts repentance, the Most Merciful.'[8]

On a serious note, this horrifically visual metaphor really drives the point home that 'backbiting,' or speaking negatively about someone in his or her absence, is a pretty awful sin. In Islam, as in some other spiritual traditions, we believe that when we say something negative about a person in their absence, on the Day of Recompense, we take on their sins and they take on our good actions.

This applies even if what we're saying about the person is true. If we lie as well as say something negative, it's classed as slander, which is even more harmful. The Prophet Muhammad, peace and blessings upon him, said:

> *'Do you know what backbiting is?*
> *It is to say something about your brother that he would dislike.'*

Someone asked him, 'But what if what I say is true?' The Messenger of God, peace and blessings upon him, replied:

'If what you say about him is true, you are backbiting him, but if it is not true then you have slandered him.'[9]

The nature of a true believer is such that the more you spend time with them, the more they speak and do good to you – so the more your soul is inclined to love them. If we're with a friend and he or she speaks negatively about those who aren't present, it's quite likely that he or she will do the same to us when we're not there. If you never hear a negative word from your friend about others, be assured that in your absence, he or she likely protects you in the same way.

Flesh-eating media pundits

'Behold, you received it on your tongues,
and said out of your mouths things of which you had no knowledge;
and you thought it to be a light matter,
while it was most serious in the sight of Allah.'[10]
QURAN

One of the terribly ironic things about today's discourse on Islam is that people slander the best of creation, peace and blessings upon him. When those of us who know and love him protest, we're accused of not believing in 'free speech.' Of course we believe in free speech – we use it every day. We also believe that the worst possible way anyone could use his or her freedom of speech is to lie while insulting our beloved.

'The majority of a man's sins
emanate from his tongue.'[11]

THE PROPHET MUHAMMAD, PEACE AND BLESSINGS UPON HIM

Here's the ironic part: you've learnt how backbiting causes us to take on the sins of the one we're insulting. The Prophet, peace and blessings upon him, lived in such a way as to be completely free from all sin. He literally has no sins to give to those who insult him. Although they don't realize it, he's being merciful to them, even in his absence, and even as they insult him. He truly is a 'mercy to all the worlds,' peace and blessings upon him.

Just to be clear: the problem with insulting the Prophet, peace and blessings upon him, or Islam, is not that we Muslims may be 'offended.' The problem is that the claims people make are objectively untrue. Their words don't have the power to hurt our feelings, as our feelings can only come from Allah, via the power of thought. However, their untrue words do have the power to harm their own souls. As the Messenger of Allah, peace and blessings upon him, put it:

'A person has done enough wrong in his life if
he simply repeats everything he hears.'[12]

'Allah has never dignified anyone due to his ignorance,
nor humiliated anyone due to his forbearance.'[13]

How foolish it is to insult the one who never insulted anyone; to ridicule the one who never ridiculed anyone; to lie about the one who never lied to anyone; to wish ill upon the one who wished goodness for everyone, even the ill-wisher. May Allah guide all of us to speak only that which is true, and necessary, and kind – as we were taught by the one who always did so; may the peace, love, and blessings of Allah be upon him.

As believers, how are we to respond to those who ignorantly insult our beloved? The answer is crystal clear in the Quran:

> 'And when they hear idle talk they turn aside from it and say:
> We shall have our deeds and you shall have your deeds;
> peace be on you, we do not desire the ignorant.'[14]

CHAPTER 11

Resilience – the Greatest Virtue

'Dear Believers, seek help through resilience and prayer. Indeed Allah is with the resilient.'[1]

QURAN

If there's one virtue that Muslims aim to live up to and demonstrate in an exemplary manner, it's the virtue of '*sabr*.' This Arabic word is sometimes translated as 'patience,' 'perseverance,' 'persistence,' or 'steadfastness,' although it has a deeper meaning. It's to persevere on the right path, even under the most adverse circumstances. My preferred translation of *sabr* therefore is 'resilience.'

Sabr is to continue to do good actions, personally and collectively – specifically when facing opposition or encountering problems and setbacks, or when facing unexpected, unwanted results. In Islam, it's considered a great blessing to be granted the virtue of *sabr*. I consider it the greatest of all virtues because the Prophet, peace and blessings upon him, said:

'No one has ever been given anything better than sabr.'[2]

Sabr is mentioned nearly 100 times in the Quran and is linked with prayer and faith itself:

'Be resilient, for your resilience is with the help
of Allah.'[3]
'Be resilient – for the Promise of Allah is true.
And ask forgiveness for your faults,
and celebrate the praises of your Lord,
in the evening and in the morning.'[4]

The twin qualities of faith

Sabr is considered the twin quality of '*shukr*,' which is gratitude. There's an understanding that as we increase in resilience, so our capacity for gratitude increases. As we increase in gratitude, our capacity for resilience increases. The Prophet, peace and blessings upon him, said:

'Amazing is the affair of the believer.
For him, there is good in all his affairs,
and this is so only for the believer.

'When something pleasing happens to him, he is grateful,
and that is good for him;

'And when something displeasing happens to him, he is resilient, and that is good for him.'[5]

Because it's performed consistently – five times a day, no matter what – prayer itself becomes a profound expression of *sabr* (resilience) or *shukr* (gratitude), or both. We pray whether we feel like it or not; whether we're high or low; in good times or bad. In doing so, the prayer becomes an elegant demonstration that, whatever life throws at us, we're ready to serve Allah, the Most Gracious. True prayer makes us grateful for the highs of life, and graceful in the lows.

Inside-Out: the Paradigm of Resilience

'Dear Believers, seek help through patience and prayer.
Indeed, Allah is with the patient.
And do not say about those who are killed in the way of Allah,
"They are dead." Rather, they are alive, but you perceive it not.
And We will surely test you with something of fear and hunger
and a loss of wealth and lives and fruits,
but give good tidings to the resilient.
Those who, when disaster strikes them, say,
"To Allah we belong, and to Him is our return."
Those are the ones upon whom are blessings and mercy from their Lord.

> And it is they who are truly guided.'[6]
>
> QURAN

The Inside-Out Paradigm has – interestingly enough – been referred to as the 'Psychological Paradigm of Resilience.' This is because of the almost endless supply of resilience we find when we know that the adversities we face are not the cause of our feelings. Perhaps the greatest blessing I ever received in my life was a deep understanding of the Inside-Out Paradigm, before the time came when I needed it.

I was awoken suddenly in the middle of the night by my father, and instantly knew what must have happened. We'd spent the last few days near the hospital in London where my sister was being treated for a liver problem. The doctor had called us because she believed my sister wouldn't make it through the night.

We arrived at Sonia's room, and the doctor told us to call any other relatives who needed to be there – my brother and aunt were on their way from Manchester. My father, sister, and mother were standing around Sonia, who lay in a coma. We all prayed for her silently. Her heartbeat got stronger as we prayed more intensely.

When everyone had arrived, I started reciting *Surah Yasin* (the 36th chapter, or *surah*, of the Quran) quietly. My father, who normally insists that we keep our religion to ourselves, told me to raise my voice. I recited all the way to the end, and as

I did so, Sonia's heartbeat, a beeping on the machine, slowed down as the recitation ended with these words from the Quran:

> 'His command is that when He intends a thing, He says to it,
> "Be," and it is.
>
> 'So exalted is He in whose hand is the control of all things,
> and to Him you will be returned.'[7]

As I reached the last verse, the machine indicated that Sonia's heart had stopped, and her face indicated that her soul had left her body. We were all in shock, and the reality of the verse we'd recited hundreds of times before entered us: 'To Allah we belong, and to Him is our return.'[8]

When tragedy strikes (and it will)

You'll notice that this is the instant response of a Muslim when they hear that someone has passed away, or that a tragedy has occurred. It doesn't take us by surprise, or damage or weaken our faith. Instead, it strengthens our faith. We were guaranteed by Allah that this would happen, and it did. The loss of my sister was, of course, particularly hard for my parents. As if talking about my parents, the Prophet Muhammad, peace and blessings upon him, said:

'When a son of a servant of Allah dies, Allah Says to the angels,
"Have you taken the son of My servant?"
They say, "Yes."

'Then Allah Says, "Have you taken the fruit of his heart?"
They say, "Yes."

'Then Allah Says, "What has My servant said?"
They say, "He has praised You and said
To Allah we belong and to Him is our return."

'Then Allah Says, "Build a house for My servant in Paradise,
and call it The House of Praise."'[9]

Over the next few days, as the reality of what had happened sunk in, I made myself useful by being present for my family and helping with the arrangements. During this time, I had many insightful realizations.

I'd always believed that what happens to us, especially a tragic circumstance, has the power to dictate how we feel. I'd always believed that such a situation would necessarily make everyone involved feel a certain way. I'd always believed that if someone I loved were to pass away, I would feel unbearable sadness. I'd always been wrong.

The fact that feeling comes from the thought we're in, not the circumstance we're in, was visibly demonstrated to me in the week after Sonia passed away, may Allah immerse her in an abundance of mercy and light.

The fact is, every individual in my family, myself included, was feeling different from everyone else. And everyone's mood changed from moment to moment. My sister was stressed, my father was angry, my mother was sad, and my brother felt guilty. Each of us was living in our own thought-generated separate reality. We're each, always, in our own 'world.' I realized that this is, perhaps, one meaning of the beginning of *Surah al-Fatiha*:

> 'All praise and gratitude is due to Allah, Lord of all the worlds.'[10]
>
> QURAN

Death and coffee

The day after my sister's funeral, almost everyone we knew came to our house to pay their respects to her, as is customary in Muslim culture. I've noticed that in some European cultures, when a person dies, the protocol is to leave the bereaved alone because they might need time to grieve. This is well intentioned, but I'm not sure it helps. Death can become a taboo, and the bereaved often don't know who to talk to or what to make of it, especially as society becomes less religious and spiritual.

'Remember death, 20 times a day.'[11]

THE PROPHET MUHAMMAD, PEACE AND BLESSINGS UPON HIM

I've heard that there are now 'death cafés' where people can go, drink coffee, and openly talk about their feelings of grief and loss. Although it can make for awkward conversation and even more awkward silences, I believe it's always better to visit those in grief than to let them figure it out on their own. For Muslims, when someone dies, absolutely everyone, near and far, comes to visit and food is arranged by other families to make life easier for those who are grieving the most.

One thought away

Because so many people were visiting our house, and because it was a time for mourning, a preacher was invited to give a talk. However, his talk didn't quite console anyone, and he was somewhat off-key, as preachers can be sometimes. It occurred to my older brother that the next day, I should give the talk, as it might be more meaningful for some of our family members.

The essence of my talk was simple, and it was the best advice I could give to anyone. Much as I do in this book, I shared some beautiful verses of the Quran and Prophetic teachings, and the point I made was that our feelings come from the spiritual gift of thought, moment by moment, not from the situation we're in.

This doesn't mean that our sadness isn't real. But it does mean that no matter how intense our sadness gets, we're only ever one thought away from being happy again. This concept was so simple that my sister Sonia's three beautiful, brilliant daughters all understood it instantly. May Allah immerse them all in light, guidance, and spiritual wisdom.

I told them directly: you're going to think sad thoughts and feel very sad in some moments. But you're only ever going to be one thought away from thinking happy thoughts, and returning to happiness again, in other moments. This understanding is the epitome of mental health and the endless fountain of resilience.

From positive thinking to peaceful sadness

How we feel can't come from a tragedy. How we feel comes directly from the God-given power of thought. Knowing that I could only feel my thinking, and that I don't always have control over my thinking, was a huge relief. I didn't need to get rid of the feeling of sadness, or 'positive think' my way out of it. Instead, I understood where my feelings were actually coming from.

I gave myself permission to break down into tears at any moment, or to be neutral, or even to have a happy memory and laugh in any moment. Knowing that all of this could happen brought a surprising amount of freedom. As a result I was calm and resilient, which was a sparse but valuable resource during such a time. I was still sad for some of the time, often in prayer, but the sadness had a different quality to it that I had not previously known was possible.

There's a great difference between feeling sad about a tragedy while knowing that the sadness is coming from the way we're thinking in the moment, and feeling sad about a tragedy while falsely believing that the tragedy itself is the cause of our sadness.

If I'm sad, and I'm absolutely convinced that the tragedy is the cause of my sadness, there's no hope for me to ever feel better. My mind is closed to the possibility of insight, or new, more uplifting perspectives. I'm taking thought out of the equation. And, in reality, I'm taking the spiritual nature of my self and the Infinite Power of Allah to make me feel better at any moment, out of the equation.

I'm not aware that my feelings are in Allah's hands, and I'm using my imagination to put my feelings in the hands of the tragedy. I'm lost in the illusion. As a result, the sadness gets deeper and can turn into an unbearable kind of depression. The whole experience is devoid of *sabr*.

If, on the other hand, I'm sad and I absolutely know that Allah, via thought in the moment, is the cause of my sadness, externally nothing has changed but internally everything is different. I know that I could feel better at any moment, because just as easily as I fell into sad thinking, I could fall into happy thinking. My mind is open to the possibility of insight – of seeing the situation from a deeper perspective.

I'm putting thought back into the equation. I'm putting the spiritual nature of my self and the Infinite Power of Allah to determine my felt experience, back into the equation. Even though the feeling of sadness may still be there, it's now a richer, more meaningful kind of sadness. It's now 'Peaceful Sadness' – a sadness with a deep, rich connection to Allah, which we would happily, gracefully bear for as long as Allah wills. This is the meaning of *sabr*.

There's nothing I would have liked more than to share this understanding with my sister Sonia, may the peace, love, blessings, and forgiveness of Allah descend upon her, in abundance. It would no doubt have had a powerfully positive impact on her life. Although I couldn't share the Inside-Out with Sonia, I can dedicate my life to sharing it with all of my other sisters, and brothers, in Islam, and in humanity. *Insha'Allah* (God willing).

Let's end this chapter with a recitation of *Surah al-Fatiha* for my sister:

> 'In the name of Allah, the Most Kind, the Most Loving;
> All gratitude and praise is due to Allah, Lord of all the worlds;
> The Most Kind, the Most Loving,
> Master of the Day of Recompense,
> You alone we worship; You alone we ask for help.
> Guide us to the Straight Path
> The path of those you have blessed;
> those who incur no anger, and who have not gone astray.
> Ameen.'

CHAPTER 12

Inspired Action – the Fruit of Belief

'Indeed we created humans in the best of forms,
then we reduced them to the lowest of the low;
except for those who believe and do good actions –
for them is a never-ending reward.'[1]

QURAN

The terms 'believe' and 'do good actions' are put together in a phrase that's repeated in the Quran more than 100 times. The implication is that, if someone truly believes in Allah and the Last Day, they will do nothing but good actions toward their neighbors and humanity, as much as they can. Frequently, after the phrase 'believe and do good actions,' comes a description of its reward: Paradise.

For believers, the objective in life is to do as much good as possible in the short time we have here on Earth. In one respect, it's the very purpose of life. As the Quran puts it:

> 'The One who created death and life, to test which of you is most excellent in action, And He is the Almighty, the Most Forgiving.'[2]

'*Iman*,' which in this book I've translated as 'belief,' is a deeply spiritual concept, and the source of gratitude and resilience. It's much more than an intellectual idea that we're holding onto, as the English word 'belief' might suggest. Rather, it's a kind of spiritual energy that overtakes us when we're aligned with truth.

Action from the spirit

By putting the terms 'believe' and 'do good actions' together, we find that there's a spiritual quality to the action that runs deeper than the action itself. So for example, it's not just to give to charity, but to *believe* and to give to charity.

To believe that Allah is watching you as you give; to believe that it will make a difference; to believe that giving increases your wealth, and never decreases it; to believe that what you give will come back to you manifold; to believe that your wealth is completely from Allah, anyway; to believe that the person, or cause, is worth it, and to believe in the soul of humanity.

The following is a beautiful, sacred saying of the Prophet that will give you an idea of how belief in Allah and the Afterlife beautifully tie in with noble actions. The Prophet, peace and blessings upon him, said:

'Allah will say on the Day of Judgment: "Son of Adam, I was sick but you did not visit Me." The servant will reply: "My Lord, How could I visit You when You are the Lord of the Worlds?" Allah will respond: "Did you not know that one of My servants was sick and you didn't visit him? If you had visited him you would have found Me there."

'Then Allah will say: "Son of Adam, I needed food but you did not feed Me." The servant will ask: "My Lord, How could I feed You when You are the Lord of the Worlds?" Allah will say: "Did you not know that one of My servants was hungry but you did not feed him? If you had fed him you would have found its reward with Me."

'Then Allah will say: "Son of Adam, I was thirsty, but you did not give Me something to drink." The servant will reply: "My Lord, How could I give a drink when You are the Lord of the Worlds?" Allah will say: "Did you not know that one of My servants was thirsty but you did not give him a drink? If you had given him a drink, you would have found its reward with Me."'[3]

From a purely materialistic perspective, we could rationalize our way out of any good action, as our measurement is purely in terms of the net material effect. From a spiritual perspective, based on the knowledge that Allah exists and is creating our reality moment by moment, we do good from a different place. This is what 'inspired action' refers to: action from the spirit.

A glimpse into the 'body' of Islam

Technically, the form of the good actions we take falls under the 'body' of Islam, as they are outward practices. The depth of intention and the love with which we do the actions are the 'soul' of Islam. In reality, the Quran doesn't separate out the body, mind, and soul of Islam, or the practices, beliefs, and spirituality. One verse will often contain deep insights into all three dimensions.

'Good actions' is a general term in the Quran and Sunnah that encompasses literally all good works. It includes personal worship, charity, and any and all forms of education, self-improvement, integrity, keeping promises and contracts, mending family ties, being good to parents, social work, and being of benefit to human beings and all of creation.

The definition of 'goodness' is given in a Quran verse that was revealed in an interesting historical context. The Prophet, peace and blessings upon him, was originally commanded to make the direction of prayer the East, toward Masjid al-Aqsa in Jerusalem. At a certain point, the direction was changed to the Kaba in Mecca.

At the time, opponents of Islam mocked the Muslims and the Prophet, peace and blessings upon him, for not knowing which way they should face when they pray. In response, this Quran verse was revealed:

'Goodness does not consist in turning your face toward East or West.
The truly good are those who believe in Allah and the Last Day,
in the angels, the scripture, and the prophets;
'Who give away some of their wealth, however much they cherish it,
to their relatives, to orphans, the needy, travelers, and beggars,
and to liberate those in bondage;
'Those who keep up the prayer and pay the prescribed alms;
who keep pledges whenever they make them;
'Those who are resilient in misfortune, adversity, and times of danger.
These are the ones who are true, and conscious of Allah.'[4]

Here are a few of the many beautiful statements of the Prophet, peace and blessings upon him, that encourage us to focus on good actions. These statements had a huge influence on Muslim cultures in different parts of the world.

'Dear People, you should do whatever good deeds you can,
for Allah does not get tired [of giving reward] until you get tired.
The most beloved of good deeds to Allah are those
in which a person persists, even if they are few.'[5]

'Gabriel [has] advised me to do good to my neighbors so frequently that I thought he would have me make my neighbors the heir to my inheritance.'[6]

'The one who sleeps while his neighbor is hungry is not a believer.'[7]

'Allah loves to see His servant exhausted after an honest day's work.'[8]

'Once, a person approached the Prophet (peace and blessings upon him) and asked: "O Prophet of Allah! Toward whom should I exhibit goodness and kindness?" He replied: "Toward your mother."

'The man then asked: "And after that toward whom?" He replied: "Your mother."

'He asked again: "And then?" He replied: "Your mother."

'For the fourth time, the man asked: "And then?" This time he said: "Your father."'[9]

'To bring about justice between two is an act of charity. To help a man get on his mount, lifting him onto it, or helping him put his belongings onto it, is an act of charity.'[10]

Knowledge, action, results

As we discovered in Chapter 5, in Islam, 'faith' or 'belief' is rooted in, and inextricably bound with, knowledge, which causes an upward spiral: knowledge leads to faith, which leads to good action. One of the best actions is to increase in beneficial knowledge, and the fruit of this is… more good action.

As a coach, I sometimes help other coaches – especially those who use the Inside-Out Paradigm to transform people's lives – to grow their practices too. I've studied several business growth methods that work, and successfully implemented them. When I look at my students, I can very clearly see the real-world benefits of this spiritual understanding of inspired action.

If we study how to grow a business, but never take action, we won't see the fruits of that study – it won't result in new clients. If, on the other hand, we blindly take action without first studying business growth methods, we could waste time, money, and energy, and still not see the fruits of that action.

Islam teaches us that truly 'inspired action' requires both. True knowledge feeds the mind and spirit and the body responds with action. The fruits that come from this are delicious and abundant. In the following powerful statement, al-Ghazali, may Allah be pleased with him, a twelfth-century master of the Islamic tradition, summarizes this understanding:

'Action without knowledge is in vain.
Knowledge without action is insane.'[11]

What's your come-from?

All of us sometimes, internally, come from a place of arrogance, ignorance, misunderstanding, desperation, and ingratitude. This is to be afflicted with the 'spiritual diseases of the heart' that make our actions internally impure, even if they appear to be externally 'good.'

In other words, we're all, sometimes, in denial and Outside-In. Like the desperately needy business owner who thinks more clients will make her feel better, or the desperately needy single person who thinks love and happiness will come from finding a partner.

Sometimes we all come from a place of sincerity, love, understanding, resilience, and gratitude. This is to be blessed with a 'sound heart,' which makes our actions internally pure, even if they appear to be externally questionable. In other words, we are all, sometimes, aligned with the truth of the Inside-Out.

This is to be like the confident, inspiring business owner who's naturally attractive to clients because she knows she doesn't need them to feel gratitude and abundance; or the confident, inspiring single man who knows that all the love and happiness he needs is already within him and comes from Allah.

As people, we tend to judge and think in terms of the external actions and results, as we don't look inward, and can't see into each heart, or where we're coming from. However,

Allah looks at both. As the Prophet, peace and blessings upon him, said:

'Indeed Allah does not look at your appearance, or image, but looks into your hearts and at your actions.'[12]

Similarly, the Quran says:

'Nothing will benefit them on that Day:
Not their children; nor their wealth,
Except the one who brings forth a sound heart.'[13]

Actions and intentions

It's made clear in Islam that one could engage in actions that appear to be good but come from a place of impure intention ('*niya*'), making the action unrewardable. Similarly, an action done with a clear, pure intention carries spiritual power. The Prophet, peace and blessings upon him, said:

'Actions are according to intentions,
and everyone will get what they intended.
Whoever migrates for Allah and His Messenger,
their migration will be for Allah and His Messenger.

'Whoever migrates for worldly gain, or to marry a woman,
then his migration will be for the sake
of whatever he migrated for.'[14]

The key here is how deep we're willing to go to understand our real intentions. I realized after seeing the truth of the Inside-Out understanding that many (perhaps most) of my actions were for the sake of attaining or avoiding feelings.

They were rooted in a misunderstanding of where feelings actually come from, and although I wasn't consciously aware of it, almost everything I did – including prayer itself – was in the hope of feeling better. I would pray because I didn't want to feel guilty. I would give charity to others because I wanted the feeling of being a 'generous' person.

However, after the Inside-Out understanding, I could see that these actions can't, in reality, give me the feelings I want – only Allah can, and Allah doesn't need me to do anything to make me feel a certain way. Rather, Allah has set up a system: you'll only ever feel the way you think.

Before this realization, I'd always believed that my intentions in doing good works were always pure. After this humbling realization, I clearly saw that whenever I'm caught up in the Outside-In, no matter how hard I work, my intentions are for feelings, not for Allah. It reminds me of the following famous Prophetic teaching:

'A scholar is asked by Allah, "What did you do with the blessings we gave you?" He replied, "I studied sacred knowledge and taught it for your sake."

'Allah responds: "You are lying! You studied sacred knowledge so people would call you a knowledgeable man, and they did. You received your reward. Now Hell is your abode."'[15]

Inspired action is the fruit of sound belief. Such actions, done from the Inside-Out with the best of intentions and purely for Allah, carry immense spiritual power and impact, even if they are few.

It's said that a handful of the Prophet's companions engaged in relatively few inspired actions, but with such heart, such intensity, such purity of intention, and such deep knowledge of the sacred, that the impact was such that the adherents of Islam now number more than one billion. This is 'inspired action,' which is the fruit of 'belief' and alignment with truth.

I will end with a short, succinct chapter of the Quran that summarizes our learning about Truth, Resilience, and Inspired Action:

'In the name of Allah, the Most Loving, the Most Kind;
By Time – Surely mankind are at loss;
Except for those who believe and do good actions,
And encourage each other toward Truth,
And encourage each other to be resilient.'[16]

CHAPTER 13

Gratitude – the Source of Abundance

'And among His signs is this:
That He sends the winds as glad tidings,
giving you a taste of His Mercy,
and that the ships may sail at His command,
and that you may seek of His Bounty,
in order that you may be thankful.'[1]

QURAN

When we ask someone how they are, the usual response is something like 'Good,' 'Fine,' 'Alright.' The Islamic response, which you'll hear all over the Muslim world, is '*alhamdulillah*,' which means 'all gratitude and praise is due to Allah.'

This phrase may be familiar to you, as it occurs at the very beginning of the first chapter of the Quran, which we recite in every prayer. Every one of our five daily prayers is a deliberate expression of gratitude to the One who inspired us to pray. In the beautiful *Adhan* ('call to prayer') – which you'll hear in any Muslim city, five times a day – one of the verses is: 'Come to prayer; come to success.'

Prayer itself is considered success. And from the very first words the prayers are filled with love and gratitude. Perhaps success is gratitude in and of itself. Gratitude, like *dhikr* (remembrance of Allah), is an end in itself. The blessings we've been granted are there for the purpose of inspiring gratitude within us. The default position is to let gratitude for life itself wash over us and to let our tongue respond with words of praise. This is the spiritual path.

On one occasion, Aisha, the wife of the Prophet, may Allah be pleased with her, found him standing in prayer in the middle of the night, as he often did for hours on end. She asked him:

> *'O Prophet of Allah, why do you undergo so much hardship despite the fact that Allah has pardoned for you your earlier and later sins?' He responded, "Should I not, then, be a grateful servant?"'*[2]

What are you most grateful for today?

I often start group coaching sessions with this question. In almost every session, there's one person who answers it with 'Nothing,' and another who says 'Everything.' In any given moment, without the 'things' of our lives changing, we can either be immensely grateful for what we've got, or frustrated because we don't have more.

A scholar told me of a friend of his who was a very wise Muslim and a quadriplegic. This man, despite not having arms and legs – blessings I take for granted almost every day – was always in a constant state of gratitude and saying *alhamdulillah.*

One day something less than pleasant and quite inconvenient happened to him, and in response, he just increased his praise of Allah. His wife, a little exasperated, asked him, 'Look at what happened to you – why are you still saying *alhamdulillah*?' The wise man replied, 'I'm saying *alhamdulillah* because Allah guided me to say *alhamdulillah.*' I can't knock that logic.

Gratitude, like all feelings and attitudes, doesn't require an object. There doesn't have to be a 'thing' for which you're grateful. The Prophet, peace and blessings upon him, taught us that every joint and bone is a blessing for which we ought to feel so grateful that we should give to charity as a way of thanking Allah:

> *'On every person's joints or small bones, there is charity due every day the Sun rises. Doing justice between two people is charity; assisting a man to mount his animal, or lifting up his belongings onto it, is charity; a good word is charity; every step you take toward prayer is charity; and removing harmful things from pathways is charity.'*[3]

When we're in this state, it's possible to look at virtually anything and see it in a grateful way. It's like seeing the world through 'gratitude goggles.' Through the power of thought, we can be grateful just for the sake of it; just for the mere fact of being able to be grateful; just for the fact that we're experiencing all of reality through the God-given miracle of thought, right now, in this moment.

The secret to abundance

> 'Be grateful and Allah will give you more.'[4]
>
> Quran

This verse of the Quran contains the simple secret to abundance. The more we're grateful for the blessings we have, the more Allah blesses us with, by His Infinite Generosity. For each moment of presence and awareness in which we're grateful to Allah, we're actually rewarded eternally.

Christian Mickelsen, one of my business mentors, has become a good friend. He's an inspiring business leader and coach, and many years ago, he showed me the ins and outs of growing a coaching business. At a certain point, however, he hit a plateau in his own business. (I say 'plateau,' but in truth, his plateau would be like hitting the jackpot for most of us!)

He solved this problem in the same congruent way he solved most of his problems in life, and in the same way he teaches his clients to: he hired a coach. One of the first and most noticeable changes she encouraged him to make was simply to pray, out of gratitude, before every meal. Since then, every meal I've shared with Christian has been preceded by one of us giving thanks for the food.

In that very same year, his business quadrupled, and he reached the Forbes 5,000 Fastest-Growing Companies. The energy behind real gratitude is incredibly powerful.

> 'Dear Believers, eat from the pure things
> which We have provided for you
> And be grateful to Allah,
> if it is Him that you worship.'[5]
> QURAN

We could put this down to coincidence, or find a material reason for my friend's success. He no doubt changed other things in his routine, but the biggest, most apparent change was how much more grateful he became, and that was *before* he started making any other changes. It was gratitude that stood at the base of his new routine. In Islam we say 'All "*rizq*," or "sustenance," comes from Allah.' Since food is the most real form of sustenance, being grateful for it has an incredible impact.

Expressing gratitude from the Inside-Out

I've found that there are three ways to express true gratitude:

Lose the gratitude journal

The first, as we've seen, is to express our thanks toward Allah for the gifts we've received, with our tongue. We would not even be able to experience these gifts without Allah creating our moment-to-moment experience of them, via thought. The moment we become aware of this, it's only natural to pause and say *alhamdulillah*.

One of my students, Sandie – may Allah continue to increase and reward her gratitude, insight, and wisdom – used to wake at 5 a.m. every day to write an entry in her 'gratitude journal.' After discovering the Inside-Out Paradigm she no longer found it necessary to 'do' gratitude as a practice. Instead, she now finds herself being in complete awe of the divine every time she remembers where her feelings come from. She doesn't keep a gratitude journal any more, but she assures me she has never in her life felt such a depth of gratitude.

Before understanding the Inside-Out Paradigm, Sandie was trying to *make* herself feel grateful, because it sounded like a good idea. Since receiving this understanding, she's been overwhelmed with gratitude for the very fact that feeling comes from thought in the moment. What a relief it is to wake up every morning saying 'thank you' when you really feel it. This is real gratitude from the heart *and* the tongue, not just the tongue.

'Remember Me and I will remember you.
And be grateful to Me and not ungrateful.'[6]
QURAN

Love what you've got

The second way we can express true gratitude is to joyfully and lovingly use the gifts we receive in life. While driving home from the mosque one day, I had the thought that I'd really love to be a *hafidh* of the Quran – someone who has memorized it all. Then I realized that if I were a *hafidh*, the only difference it would make to me right now is that the whole Quran would be inside of me and I'd be able to recite it.

Then the penny dropped. I *already* have some of the Quran inside of me! If I want Allah to bless me with more, the least I can do is be grateful for what I've already got – and what better way to be grateful than to use that gift by reciting it right now? If I don't recite what I know of the Quran now, what makes me think I'll recite what I learn in the future?

Without frequent recitation, it's almost as if the whole Quran would be wasted on me. From that moment on, any time I have the inspiring wish to become a *hafidh*, I just start reciting what I know of the Quran, with deep gratitude for how much Allah has blessed me with. The best way to be grateful is by lovingly using the gifts we receive, from anyone, right there and then.

Clients often ask me how they can 'get' more insight. Insight is a divine gift that Allah bestows on who He wants, when He wants. There's nothing we can do to 'make Allah' speed it up, or slow it down. It's completely out of our control.

However, just as being grateful for the Quran is the best approach to take if you want to be blessed with more of it, so being grateful for the spiritual insights and divine guidance you've received up to this point in your life is the best approach if you want more of them. If you think you haven't been blessed with guidance in your life until now, think again. Guidance is everywhere. Like the path that brought you to this moment, reading this book.

Enjoy paying the bills

The third way to express gratitude is to pay and thank the people who brought the gift to us. The Prophet, peace and blessings upon him, said:

> *'He who has not thanked people has not thanked Allah.'*[7]

We can thank people through loving actions, by genuinely feeling gratitude for the gift, and by saying 'thank you' from the heart. Muslims give thanks with the words '*Jazak Allah Khair*,' or 'May Allah give you the best of rewards.'

Sometimes we express our gratitude in words, and at other times by literally paying for it, to reciprocate. The payment doesn't replace gratitude. Instead, the payment is a symbolic representation of how much we value the object or service.

When it comes to bills, rather than feeling stressed or frustrated that we 'have to' pay them, we could take a moment to bring to mind what each one is actually for (heating; running water; the home we live in; the taxes that keep our country running). There are three things to be grateful for as we pay a bill:

- The value that we receive, which the bill represents.
- The fact that Allah has blessed us with enough money to pay the bill (or for the fact that we can logistically figure out how to pay it over time).
- The fact that we're alive, right now, in this moment, having the whole thought-generated experience. From an Islamic perspective, we're engaging in a praiseworthy, eternally rewardable action: fulfilling a commitment to pay for a service or product we've received.

By paying a bill with this energy of gratefulness *insha'Allah* (God willing), more '*baraka*,' or 'divine blessing,' is infused into our wealth, and we're being abundant. In fact, when someone pays us for our products or services, the Prophetic prayer we make for them is this: 'May Allah put *baraka* into your wealth.'

Another completely counterintuitive way to express our gratitude, which also increases our wealth and abundance, is as follows.

The 'other' secret to abundance

> 'Who will give Allah a good loan, which He will increase for him many times over?
> It is Allah who withholds and Allah who gives abundantly, and it is to Him that you will return.'[8]
>
> Quran

> 'Say: My Lord gives in abundance to whichever of His
> servants He will, and sparingly to whichever He will;
> He will replace whatever you give in alms.
> He is the Best of Providers.'[9]
>
> Quran

One of the defining qualities of a believer is that we give abundantly to those in need. We do this because we know that our wealth comes from Allah, and we're promised that Allah will increase it, if we spend it on the needy. This is one of the most obvious and beautiful forms of the 'good actions' we looked at in Chapter 12.

Muslims are taught (and repeatedly reminded at every single charity fundraiser) that spending in the way of Allah by giving to the needy doesn't decrease our wealth but actually increases it. We don't take our wealth and savings with us to a next life, as the Egyptian pharaohs believed, but we believe that it's our good actions that we take with us: the more we give, the more we receive. We're also taught that this is the 'best of deals,' as Allah will repay us manifold in this life and in the Eternal Life to come.

The more we 'spend out of that which We have given you,' as the Quran puts it, the more we're proving our gratitude for that which has been granted, and plugging into the flow of abundance that's all around us.

The more we 'give God a good loan, which He will increase…', as the Quran puts it, the more we're proving our gratitude for that which has been granted, and plugging into the flow of abundance that's all around us. These verses are the foundation of the success of many successful global charity and aid organizations, and the inspiration of many grateful, abundant and generous individuals.

'Thanksgiving is sweeter than bounty itself.
One who cherishes gratitude does not cling to the gift!
Thanksgiving is the true meat of Allah's bounty;
the bounty is its shell,
For thanksgiving carries you to the heart of the Beloved…'

Rumi

CHAPTER 14

Jihad – the Universal Human Value

'O Divine Bird! Dying is better than that which stops you flying.'

Muhammad Iqbal

Like all believing Muslims, I believe in *jihad*. It's an intrinsic part of Islam. Often, when spiritual or liberal Muslims talk about the 'j-word,' it's assumed that they believe in a watered-down, personal, 'spiritual *jihad*.' I believe in the inner, spiritual *jihad* against the '*nafs*' (ego) every bit as much as I believe in the combative *jihad* against an actual enemy. (I talk about these two forms of *jihad* later in this chapter.)

In today's world, my assertion might raise an eyebrow or two. When I ask my non-Muslim friends what they think *jihad* means, they almost always say 'holy war.' Let's take a moment to explore this.

The Arabic word for 'holy' is '*qudus*' and the Arabic word for 'war' is '*harb*.' So, if we were to translate the term 'holy war' back into Arabic, we'd end up with '*harb qudsy*.' And as one of my American friends would say, that's not a thing! So, we're off to a shaky start. But let's keep going.

Scary Arabic words

You may have noticed that every other chapter in Part II of this book has started with an Arabic word or term, followed by its definition or meaning. That's because I'm cognizant of the fact that most readers of this book aren't fluent in classic Arabic and will appreciate this information.

The word *jihad* has just as deep a linguistic and spiritual significance as every other Arabic word featured in this book. However, have you noticed that, so far, you've been reading the word *jihad* without needing to have it defined? That's because it's been incorporated into the English language, but sadly, without the correct meaning.

Jihad is not alone in this. Over the years we've see this mechanism imposed on many Arabic words. They become part of the English language but in the process their meaning is changed to something much more sinister, and much less spiritual, than that implied by the original. Aside from *jihad* these include common words such as Islam (peaceful acceptance or surrender, and the name of the religion that Muslims follow), and *Shariah* (the Way or Path).

These Arabic terms have clear, specific, and deep meanings that become completely lost when they are incorporated into

English, and employed by mass-media outlets that don't take the time for the nuances of translation and localization.

One of my favorite books is *The Way of the Peaceful Warrior* by Dan Millman. It's about a gymnast who finds inner peace with the help of a mysterious spiritual teacher. It's a wonderful read, and Hollywood made a movie based on the book. One day, as I was reading the book while traveling on the London Underground, something struck me. If, instead, the book I was reading was called *The Shariah of the Islamic Jihadi* – which is a feasible translation – that title wouldn't seem quite so peaceable and I might not make it to my destination without giving a free Arabic language class to the police.

What does *jihad* actually mean?

So, without further ado, let's answer this question. *Jihad* is the verbal noun of the trilateral root word '*jahada*,' which means 'to struggle.' The Arabic word has both a literal and a spiritual significance for Muslims. To 'do *jihad*' is to 'struggle' to do something worthwhile or good, even though it's intrinsically difficult. If the task is easy, it wouldn't be considered *jihad*.

Jihad is a human value that virtually all of humanity already believes in. Most people just don't know that this is what it's called in Arabic. We all know that the easy, instant-gratification option probably won't work out well for us in the long-term, and admire people who manage to overcome it.

Overcoming what's easy but bad for you, and taking the harder option that's good for you, is *jihad*.

In the most everyday, practical terms, for some of us this could mean waking up for the pre-dawn prayer, managing to meditate, or to read something beneficial every day. For others it could be eating fresh and healthy whole foods instead of unhealthy fast foods. Every working mother knows exactly what *jihad* is, and lives it, as does everyone who has a self-development plan or who has ever made the effort to go to the gym instead of sitting on the sofa watching TV.

On the other hand, there's a legitimate combative *jihad*. In a combative context, *jihad* is still a universal human value, one where someone is willing to sacrifice their own comfort, and even their own life, to save innocent lives. The Quran says, in the story of Cane and Abel:

> '...if anyone kills a person – unless in punishment for murder or mass-destruction in the land – it is as if he kills all mankind, while if any saves a life it is as if he saves the lives of all mankind. Our messengers came to them with clear signs, but many of them continued to commit excesses in the land.'[1]

If someone were to charge into the café where I'm writing this book, wielding an axe and trying to kill the people sitting around me, it would be my '*jihad*' to try and save their lives by physically stopping the assailant. The Quran says, in this respect:

'And why should you not fight in the cause of Allah and in the cause of those who, being weak, are oppressed? Men, women, and children, whose cry is: "Our Lord! Rescue us from this town, whose people are oppressors; and raise for us from thee one who will protect; and raise for us from thee one who will help!"'[2]

The rules of war in Islam

Muslims believe that the only reason the Prophet, peace and blessings upon him, was made to be in situations that could only be resolved through war, was to teach humanity the ethics of warfare. There are 10 rules of warfare in Islam; these are enshrined in the Quran and Sunnah and haven't changed in the last 1,400 years:[3]

1. Do not kill women
2. Do not kill children
3. Do not kill civilians
4. Do not kill non-combatants
5. Do not kill worshippers
6. Do not kill the elderly
7. Do not kill the sick
8. Do not destroy villages or towns
9. Do not cut down a tree
10. Do not use fire

It's also forbidden to practice treachery or mutilation, to strike the face, or to do something unethical just because one's opponent does so.[4] These rules of warfare given to us by the Prophet, peace and blessings upon him, are morally far more stringent than those used by the United Nations. By dropping a bomb, for example, most, if not all, of these rules are automatically violated.

These rules of warfare given to us by the Prophet, peace and blessings upon him, are morally far more stringent than those used by the United Nations. By dropping a bomb, for example, most, if not all, of these rules are automatically violated.

Our religion's rules of warfare are why the majority of Muslims are anti-war, and were almost unanimously opposed to the invasion of Iraq in 2003; because the war was illegal according to the fundamental spiritual and ethical teachings of Islam.

The fact that the Quran says that 'to kill one innocent life' is like destroying all of humanity means that there really isn't a justification for modern-day warfare. In an age of such technologically advanced, horrifically destructive weaponry, in essence, being a Muslim means being a peace activist.

The greater *jihad*

Although the struggle of physical combat for the noble cause of protecting innocent lives is a valid and important part of

Islam, there's something even greater: '*jihad an-nafs*' – the struggle against the ego. Once, when the Prophet, peace and blessings upon him, was walking away from a battlefield, he said:

> '*Now we leave the lesser* jihad, *for the greater* jihad.'[5]

A few months ago, I visited Morocco in North Africa and took a road trip to the Valley of the Roses – a small village in the Atlas mountains – for an annual gathering of predominantly Muslim spiritual seekers who were there to do *dhikr*. (I swear I'm not making any of this up, and yes, it was even more beautiful than it sounds.)

The nights were mostly made up of reciting the Quran and a beautiful collection of Prophetic prayers. The leader of the gathering was a spiritual master and a traditional scholar of Islam called Shaykh Mortada and one evening, he gave a particularly powerful talk after an intense session of *dhikr.*

He explained why it is that *jihad an-nafs*, or the '*jihad* against the ego,' is a 'greater' form of *jihad* than the lesser form, which is *jihad al-qital*, or 'combative *jihad*.' He gave three reasons, with the impeccable logic and depth one can expect from a scholar of his standing.

1. Combative *jihad* is strictly limited to a specific time and place, and it's for specific people. If conducted outside of this time and place, it's not acceptable to Allah and becomes

sinful. However, the spiritual *jihad* is always applicable, in every time, in every place, for everyone.

2. During combative *jihad*, one's enemy combatant is visible. In the spiritual *jihad*, one's enemy is the invisible ego. It's obviously easier, and hence less of a struggle and less rewardable, to fight a visible enemy than an invisible one.

3. If one loses a physical combative struggle against a legitimate enemy, and is killed, one goes to Heaven. If one loses the spiritual struggle against the ego, and dies, one goes to Hell. The spiritual struggle is therefore of the utmost importance and a much greater priority to all of us.

Jihad from the Inside-Out

The Inside-Out Paradigm gives us the chance to free our minds from Hell, transcend our ego, and know Allah more. It's perhaps our most valuable weapon in our most important struggle. The Outside-In Illusion – that our felt experience is coming from somewhere other than Allah, via the power of thought in the moment – is where the ego begins and ends.

The moment we see through this illusion, all of the tricks that the ego plays on us no longer work. We're awestruck by Allah's infinite presence, and the imaginings of our ego no longer overpower us. For that moment, our *jihad* is won, and with it comes the victory of spiritual realization.

Advice to Muslims who want to do *jihad*

In a beautiful video interview,[6] Shaykh Abdallah Bin Bayyah, perhaps *the* most authoritative Muslim scholar in the world today and the teacher of Shaykh Hamza Yusuf, author of *Purification of the Heart*, gave Muslims some advice about engaging in *jihad*. We pray that Allah preserves him, enables us to benefit from him, gives him strength, and increases him in all goodness, inwardly and outwardly.

The interviewer asked Shaykh Abdallah Bin Bayyah about the young Muslims who are being seduced into leaving to fight in a '*jihad*' in Syria or Iraq. This was his response:

'In the name of Allah, the Most Loving, the Most Kind. Peace and blessings upon His Prophet, his family, and companions.

'My message is that I pray to Allah, the Almighty, for them, that He guides us, and guides them. And I call on them to study the *Shariah*. If they want *jihad*, it's incumbent upon them to study the *Shariah* rules of *jihad*.

'Is what they're doing really *jihad*? Is *jihad* Muslims fighting other Muslims, and shedding the blood of innocent people? *Shariah* law has conditions, reasons, and prohibitions. For example, if a person wants to pray, could he do so in an impure, dirty place? No, his prayer would be invalid because purity is a condition of prayer.

'Can one fight for illegitimate reasons to achieve legitimate ends? This is a fight that is fundamentally illegitimate and whose results are unacceptable. So, I urge them to follow the *Shariah* law on warfare. This is not *jihad* according to *Shariah* law. This is simply war – an absurd war. A nihilistic war between Muslims with innocent lives being lost – the lives of women and children. Is this the purification of the soul? They must commit themselves to the "real *jihad*."'

The Prophet, peace and blessings upon him, said, 'A "*jihadi*" is one who strives to please Allah. Why not strive to please Allah by learning the Quran? By building mosques? By building schools? By fertilizing the earth? By helping the weak? Really, this is *jihad*. For them, this should be their *jihad*.

'And I advise them to be conscious of Allah, and I give them a piece of advice that I was given by Imam Ahmed: "Do not shed your blood and the blood of Muslims. Consider the consequences of your actions. And have *sabr*."

'That's my advice to them. That's what I see, without any vested interest. I see this as being right. I don't want them to die for no reason. I choose this for myself, my children and for them.'

There's an emphasis in this message on 'Muslims not killing Muslims,' because the vast majority – more than 90 percent – of the innocent people killed by ISIL are Muslim. Unfortunately, news of this bloodshed often doesn't make the headlines in the mainstream Western media, until Christians and Westerners are killed.

This has led some to the terrible misconception that Islam doesn't value the lives of those who believe in other religions. The following section might help clarify Islam's stance on how Muslims should treat Christians.

A message from the Prophet to Christians

The Prophet Muhammad, peace and blessings upon him, signed the following statement with his handprint. It's a letter he sent to the Christian monks of St. Catherine's Church in Mount Sinai, Egypt (or as Arabs call it, '*Jabal Musa*,' the 'Mountain of Moses,' where Moses, peace and blessings upon him, encountered the burning bush).

The letter was sent in AD628, and several certified authentic historical copies of it are available to view.

'This is a message from Muhammad ibn Abdullah,
as a covenant to those who adopt Christianity,
near and far, we are with them.

'Verily I, the servants of Allah, the helpers,
and my followers, defend them,
because Christians are my citizens;
and by Allah, I hold out against anything that displeases them.

'No compulsion is to be on them.
Neither are their judges to be removed from their jobs
nor their monks from their monasteries.

'No one is to destroy a house of their religion,
to damage it, or to carry anything from it to the Muslims' houses.
Should anyone take any of these,
he would spoil God's covenant
and disobey His Prophet.

'Verily, they are my allies and have my
secure charter against all that they hate.

'No one is to force them to travel or to oblige them to fight.
The Muslims are to fight for them.

'If a female Christian is married to a Muslim,
it is not to take place without her approval.
She is not to be prevented from visiting her church to pray.

'Their churches are to be respected.
They are neither to be prevented from repairing them,
nor the sacredness of their covenants.

'No one of the nation (of Muslims) is to disobey
the covenant until the Last Day.'[7]

So, yes. I believe in *jihad*. I strive to be a true '*jihadi*.' And may Allah accept my *jihad*. Writing this book, clarifying the basic teachings of Islam, is *jihad*. Studying and teaching the Quran is *jihad*. Studying and teaching any beneficial knowledge is *jihad*, and sharing the intrinsically beneficial knowledge of the Inside-Out Paradigm, to help alleviate needless psychological suffering, is *jihad*.

It's okay, you can admit it now. You want to do real *jihad* too. And may Allah accept it from you, and give you all the fruits and benefits of it. May Allah enable all of us to reach our potential in life, by pouring our fullest effort into serving Him and by being of benefit to His creation. As the Prophet, peace and blessings upon him, said:

> *'The best of people are those who bring the most benefit to the rest of mankind.'*[8]

CHAPTER 15

Denial – the Path of Self-Destruction

'An atheist is one who absolutely refuses to believe in a six-year-old's understanding of "God."'

Anon

It's undeniable that there's immense wisdom behind all of the verses in the Quran, not just those that sound positive. The Quran lays out two paths in life: the path of success, which is to be at peace within one's self, with the Creator, and with all of creation, and the path of self-destruction, which leads to conflict within one's self, with the Creator, and with all of creation.

What is denial?

As much as there is Heaven, there is Hell. As much as there are believers, there are those 'in denial.' Although we're rewarded for good actions, we may be punished for evil conduct. This path of self-destruction is the 'denial' (*kufr*) that the Quran repeatedly warns us about. Over and over again, the Quran alerts us to the perils of falling into denial, which is an unfortunate spiritual station that results in harmful beliefs and actions.

There are three distinct concepts that deserve attention, and must be properly understood, in order to appreciate the Quran:

1. Atheism – not believing in Allah on a purely rational basis. This category isn't mentioned in the Quran, but it's prevalent in Western society, which can lead to much confusion, which I'll aim to clarify. Atheism must not be confused with the next category.

2. *Kufr* – recognizing, then denying the truth of Allah's existence, due to spiritual diseases of the heart that result in persistent evil actions. Often (problematically) translated as simply 'disbelief.'

3. Hypocrisy – pretending to be a believer when in reality, one is in denial. The Quranic word for the one who does this is '*munafiq*.'

Before going into what it means to fall into true denial, and why this is the path to self-destruction, let's take a quick glimpse into the 'mind' of Islam and explore the idea of 'atheism.'

Atheism and irrationality

In Islam, a certain amount of knowledge is obligatory for every healthy Muslim who has come of age. This includes knowledge of the mind, body, and soul of Islam – its beliefs, practices, and spiritual values. There's a beautiful Moroccan poem called *The Helping Guide* that's learnt by children throughout North Africa in much the same way that kids in Western Europe and the USA learn nursery rhymes.

In 314 verses *The Helping Guide* combines all of the 'compulsory' basic knowledge of the belief system (mind), five pillars of practice (body), and spirituality (soul) of Islam. In fact, within the poem's first few couplets, which expound the 'mind' of Islam, the possibility of atheism is removed from the equation of the rational mind. It starts as follows (I won't even try to make this rhyme in English):

> *'A rational judgment is that which is arrived at without depending on empirical evidence or revelation.'*

The poem lays out the three ways in which knowledge can come to the human mind. The first is empirical evidence, or 'scientific inquiry.' The second is rationality: that which is understood only from logical thought. And the third is revelation: a message from God such as the Quran.

The argument for the existence of God that follows is not based on science, or divine revelation. It's based purely on rational logic. We don't need to draw on science or the Quran for this argument to work. (Whew… not bad for the first line of a nursery rhyme! It gets better…)

> *'There are three categorizations of existence: definite existence; possible existence; and impossible existence.'*

Before defining these three categories of existence, let me ask you something. In the English language, what's the opposite of 'impossible'? Is your answer, 'possible'? If so, that language trap is perhaps why atheism has become so prevalent in the English-speaking world. Let's explore this more deeply.

If something's existence is 'impossible,' then by definition, one can't rationally conceive of, or imagine, its existence. I can't give you a single example of something whose existence is impossible, by definition.

If something's existence is 'possible,' then one can rationally imagine that it might exist, or it might not exist. Everything within time, space, and matter fits into this category of 'possible' existence. Everything you can even imagine existing, like a real-life Teenage Mutant Ninja Turtle, also fits into this category of 'possible' existence. These turtles don't exist, but we can imagine them existing so they fall into the category of 'possible existence.'

However, this 'possible existence' is not the *true* opposite of 'impossible existence.' The true opposite of 'impossible existence' is what we might call 'definite existence.' It's something whose non-existence can't be imagined or rationally conceived of. Just as one can't imagine or conceive of the existence of the 'impossible,' in the same way, one can't imagine or conceive of the non-existence of the 'definite.'

Allah is definite existence. No rational person could, therefore, deny the existence of Allah. If you find this confusing, give it some time and come back to it later. (Just imagine how the Moroccan kids must feel!)

A modern-day atheist is someone who absolutely refuses to believe in a 'God' whose existence is merely 'possible.' A 'God' who exists inside of time, space, and matter. I also refuse to believe in this limited conception of God. I can't possibly fault someone for atheism, if the 'God' they've been brought up with was a magical man in the clouds. All the propositions I've heard from atheists are based on this false conception of 'God.'

The modern-day atheist is, in fact, very close to Islam. Had today's atheists been given this kind of training in rigorous, Quran-based logic at a young age, many would likely be fervent believers. Instead, most atheists are brought up with other common beliefs.

Common beliefs about God

The first common belief many people hold is that 'believers have blind faith.' Muslims don't have 'blind faith.' We believe in the unseen. There is a difference. Blind faith is superstition based on 'wishful thinking.' Belief in the unseen is based on knowledge of the divine, which can come through revelation or rationality.

The biggest myth of the postmodern world is that atheism is a more rational conclusion to arrive at than monotheism. A myth based on the saying 'We only believe in what we can see.' For the most part, this isn't true, for anyone. The truth is that we see what we've already chosen to believe.

If we believe that there's no way God can possibly exist, we'll find evidence for this everywhere. Conversely, if we believe that God must necessarily exist, we'll find evidence for this everywhere. If we believe it's impossible to know whether or not God exists, we'll find evidence for this everywhere. The choice of what to believe in precedes looking at the evidence.

Some atheists claim to 'believe in science.' It seems to me that anyone who thinks science is a belief system doesn't really understand what science is. Science is customary experience, or empirical evidence – it's a method of inquiry into truth. Why would we need to 'believe' in the evidence that we can all objectively observe?

The question is, what lies behind its existence? What conclusions are we drawing from its existence? What beliefs or philosophy are we bringing to understand the fact that it exists? Again, this completely depends on the perspective of the believer.

Atheists are believers

This is true in two ways. First and foremost, although atheism is sometimes framed as a 'non-belief,' that's philosophically untenable. Atheism is every bit as much a belief as theism. An atheist is not someone who 'does not believe in God.' An atheist is someone who *believes* that God does not exist. This is as philosophically shaky as the one who believes that God does exist, not withstanding the fact that the atheist, by definition, misunderstands what God is.

Secondly, an atheist is halfway on the journey to belief in Allah. The atheist says, '*La ilaha*' – there is no God. The believer says, '*La ilaha ila Allah*' – there is no God, except Allah. And the Muslim, acknowledging revelation, completes the saying with, '*La ilaha ila Allah, Mohammedan Rasool Allah*' – there is no God but Allah, and Muhammad is His Messenger.

How to tell if you're an 'infidel'

A friend of mine, may Allah bless her with guidance and insight, once asked me for a copy of the Quran, so I gave her my favorite translation.[1] After a couple of weeks she gave it back, saying it did nothing for her because it seemed that from the outset, it was telling her that she would go to Hell. I was very surprised at this, because that's not the way I saw it at all!

Here's the first mention of Hell in the Quran:

> 'As for those who are in denial, it makes no difference whether you warn them or not: they will not believe.
> Allah has sealed their hearts and their ears, and their eyes are covered.
> They will have great torment.'[2]

The word I'm translating here as 'in denial' is the Arabic '*kafir*.' Linguistically, the true meaning of '*kafir*' is 'the one who covers (the truth).' It's one who knows the truth but refuses to follow it, due to ignorance, arrogance, or some other disease of the heart. 'Those who are in denial' is often translated as 'disbelievers,' 'infidels,' or 'rejecters,' and sometimes 'evil-doers' or 'wrongdoers.'

Linguistically, the true opposite of '*kafir*' (one who is in denial) is '*shaakir*' (one who is grateful). The '*kafir*' is in denial of the blessings they've been given. The '*shaakir*' recognizes and is grateful for all they've been blessed with. Misunderstand what the word '*kafir*' means, and you'll inevitably misunderstand the Quran and the religion of Islam.

If you believe that you're an 'infidel' or '*kafir*,' you're essentially classing yourself – by the Quran's definition – as ignorant, arrogant, corrupt of heart, ungrateful; someone who covers up and denies the truth, and is inclined toward great evil. If you read the Quran while framing yourself as such (a disbeliever or a denier), it does something to your perspective, and your reading experience.

After this interaction with my friend, I realized that there are two ways we can understand the fact that the Quran – and Islam as a whole – are so clear and specific about 'believers who do good' and 'deniers who do evil.' There's a superficial way, which doesn't add up, and a deeper perspective, which brings clarity and light to the reader.

The superficial way to come to the Quran

The superficial, inaccurate way is to come to the Quran with a mind full of assumptions such as, 'Because I'm not a Muslim, I must be a "denier."' Or the equally problematic, 'Because I'm a Muslim, I must be a "believer."'

If we come to the Quran with this assumption, it appears to say something demonstrably untrue: that everyone who is Muslim does good and deserves Paradise, and everyone who is not Muslim does evil actions and deserves Hell. From this perspective, just because you are born a Muslim, you're chosen, through no virtue of your own, to go to Heaven, and vice versa. This is clearly inaccurate. The Quran insists that we're all raised alone, and brought to account for our own hearts and actions – irrespective of the group we belong to:

> 'On that Day, no soul will be wronged at all,
> and you will not be recompensed, except for what you used to do.'[3]

'Each soul is responsible for its own actions;
no soul will bear the burden of another.
You will all return to your Lord in the end,
and He will tell you the truth about your differences.'[4]

It's impossible that a book that is untrue, unjust, and inconsistent could possibly come from Allah, and no knowledgeable, wise, sincere person could believe in it. The religion would be reduced to blindly believing because our forefathers told us to, which is precisely what the Quran came to abolish:

'But when it is said to them, "Follow the message that
  Allah has sent down,"
they answer, "We follow the ways of our forefathers."
'What?! Even though their forefathers understood nothing
  and were not guided?'[5]

The deep way to come to the Quran

The deeper, more precise perspective, which brings a lot of clarity and light, is to come to the Quran with a clear mind, free of assumptions. That is to say: 'I don't know if I'm a "believer" or a "denier."' ('I hope, in reality, I'm a believer, but I honestly don't know.') From this humble perspective, the whole Quran suddenly speaks to the deepest part of you, and can inspire you.

The Quran then appears to say something objectively true, which is a *description, not a judgment* – one that can only be seen and given by Allah: people who do these good things are 'believers' and people who do those bad things are 'deniers.' The words 'believer' and 'denier' are thereby defined throughout the Quran by the descriptions given to each.

The Quran now speaks to a deeper part of us, because it's no longer, 'I'm a believer, lucky me,' but 'those who do all these amazing, positive things are "believers," and I hope I'm one of them.' It's not, 'I'm a "denier," but 'those who do all these horrible things are "deniers," and I hope I'm not one of them.'

It's no longer about the religion or belief system we were born into, but a moment-to-moment decision: to be at peace with creation and its Source or to be at war with creation and its Source. This is the Quranic worldview.

Part of the description of the 'denier' includes traits such as arrogant; spreads destruction; corrupt; murders without repenting. If that were an accurate description of you, I highly doubt you'd be reading this book. The Quranic descriptions of a '*kafir*' (one in denial) are clearly not an accurate description of everyone who happens not to be a Muslim. No one can easily be granted the title *kafir* – it has to be earned through a lot of terribly evil work. In the same way, one has to earn the title 'believer' by struggling to do a lot of good.

Quranic examples of *kafir* include the Pharaoh of Egypt, who persecuted the followers of Moses, and Satan, the rejected. The interesting thing about Satan – from whom we seek refuge in Allah – being a 'denier,' is that he actually knows for certain that Allah exists. Satan is not an atheist – he is a monotheist. Nonetheless, because of his arrogance in rebelling against the command of Allah and desiring evil for creation, he's classed as a *kafir* (one in denial). May Allah protect us from Satan and his traps:

> 'Has it not occurred to you, dear children of Adam, to not follow Satan?
> Indeed, he is to you, a clear enemy.
> Rather, worship Me – this is the Straight Path.'[6]
> QURAN

Hypocrisy – the worst form of denial

There's another category of '*kufr*' (denial) which, according to the Quran, is even worse. It's those who pretend to believe, when in reality they are deniers. So one could be a Muslim, but in reality a 'hypocrite' – someone who professes faith with the tongue but their heart and actions do not reflect this.

Historically, this was the case for some people who wished to sabotage the followers of the Prophet, peace and blessings upon him, by pretending to be believers. At the start of the Quran, on the third page, we're given a very precise description of this 'archetype' of the human being. As I read these verses of the Quran, it seems clear to me which infamous group of Muslims in today's world fall into this category. Then I stop for introspection, and I ask myself if I'm falling into this category.

> 'Some people say, "We believe in God and the Last Day," when really they do not believe. They seek to deceive God and the believers but they only deceive themselves, though they do not realize it. There is a disease in their hearts, to which God has added more: agonizing torment awaits them for their persistent lying.'[7]

Here, the third group is identified – they are what the Quran calls '*munafiq*' or 'hypocrite.' They claim to believe, but in reality they do not. They take on the image of Islam, but go against it with their actions. The question is: how do we know who is who? Who are the true believers and who are the 'hypocrites' who are faking? The answer is given in the next verses of the Quran:

> 'When it is said to them, "Do not cause destruction in the land," they say,
> "We are only putting things right," but really they are causing destruction, though they do not realize it.
>
> 'When it is said to them, "Believe, as the others believe," they say,
> "Should we believe as the fools do?" but they are the fools, though they do not know it.'[8]

The word 'destruction' is often translated as 'corruption'; however, it includes all major forms of wrongdoing, including murder, oppression, injustice, and crime. It includes destroying the environment, warfare without limits, and undermining the rule of law. The 'fake' believers are those who claim belief, then do such wrongdoing, as can be seen all too often on the news today. May Allah protect us all from falling into this category, protect our hearts from all spiritual diseases, and fill us with divine light and insight.

The Quran on co-existence

In the following verses, the Quran forcefully affirms that Allah exists, that the message brought by the Prophet, peace and blessings upon him, is true, and that some people won't agree with it. Which begs the question: what is the Quranic approach to dealing with people who do not believe what you believe? The answer is: stand firmly on the truth of your path, then live and let live.

> 'There is no compulsion in religion:
> true guidance has become distinct from error.'[9]

> 'In the name of Allah, the Most Loving, the Most Kind;
> Say: Dear Deniers, I do not worship what you worship;
> And you do not worship what I worship;
> And I do not worship what you worship;
> And you do not worship what I worship.
> To you your religion/way of life; to me mine.'[10]

I love how the Quran says 'and you do not worship what I worship,' indicating that, as Bob Dylan put it, you've 'gotta serve somebody.' Whether it's fortune, fame, power, or prestige, everyone is worshipping something. Most people worship the temporary things of this life, which will fade, but the believers are those who worship the Eternal, which never dies or fades.

CHAPTER 16

Psychological Idolatry – the Source of Spiritual Sickness

'There is no compulsion in religion:
true guidance has become distinct from error,
so whoever rejects false Gods and believes in Allah,
has grasped the firmest hand-hold,
one that will never break.
Allah is all hearing and all knowing.

'Allah is the ally of those who believe:
He brings them out of the depths of darkness and into the light.
As for those in denial, their allies are false gods,
who take them from the Light
into the depths of darkness...'[1]

Quran

What does it mean to take a 'false god' as an 'ally' over Allah? What does it mean to worship a false god? And why is it such a big deal? Why is it that Abraham, Moses, Jesus, and Muhammad, peace and blessings upon them all, were sent with a message that fundamentally condemns this seemingly innocent belief?

Only one God

While I was growing up, I learnt that the Quran is adamant that there's only One God, and is clear and repetitive about the fact that taking others as gods besides Allah is a grave sin. I took it in but couldn't grasp why there was such a fierce emphasis on this.

As I saw glimpses of the spiritual dimension of Islam, I realized that there must be more to it than meets the eye. After all, Abraham, peace and blessings upon him, was ostensibly an enlightened man – we can assume this from the fact that due to his intense spiritual depth, 5,000 years later we still refer to him as a prophet, peace and blessings upon him – yet, according to the biblical and Quranic accounts, he literally went into the center of town and smashed down all the idols.

How could Abraham do this, and why would he? Especially given that the *Shariah* of Islam absolutely forbids Muslims from disrespecting the beliefs of – let alone destroying the property of – any other person's religion? As if knowing that people would get this wrong, the Quran explicitly says:

'Do not insult those they call on beside Allah
in case they, in their hostility and ignorance, insult Allah.
To each community We make their own actions seem alluring,
but in the end they will return to their Lord
and He will inform them of all they did.'[2]

Psychological idolatry and the Inside-Out

It wasn't until I'd gained an understanding of the Inside-Out Paradigm that I understood why this belief that an object (the idols) has power is so detrimental. It's now clear to me why such a belief, spiritually and psychologically, is the equivalent of being taken from the 'light' into 'darkness.' And it has remarkably little to do with physically worshipping a physical idol. This is something about which the Quran is so clear; when addressing a congregation, the Prophet, peace and blessings upon him, said

'By Allah, I am not afraid that you will worship
others along with Allah after my death,
but I am afraid that you will fight
with one another for worldly things.'[3]

There's a sinister, psychological form of idolatry that we all engage in, all too often. It's the root of all of our spiritual and psychological diseases. As he often would, Sydney Banks articulated this deep concept beautifully and simply, in a couple of sentences:

> *'The sicknesses of the mind are feelings that we create and put onto objects. But if you can see the objects without the feelings, you are healthy.'*[4]

Every time we pretend that something other than Allah, the One, through some mechanism other than thought, has the power to cause our feelings, we're committing psychological idolatry. We're unwittingly using our imaginations to take the power (to cause feelings) away from Allah, and putting it in the hands of the object.

If I think a person or a situation or a thing is making me feel a certain way, in essence, I'm imagining that the thing has a power that, in reality, belongs only to Allah, the All-Powerful.

When we say the formula, 'There is no might or power except Allah,' this includes the power to cause feelings. By understanding that Allah directly causes our feelings via thought, without needing any physical object to cause them, we free our minds from the shackles of psychological idolatry and return to the truth of psychological unity. Allah becomes our ally, and we're taken 'from the darkness into the Light.'

Suddenly, all of the Quran verses about idolatry come to life and make sense. I can now see why the Quran considers it a 'terrible wrong':

'Luqman counseled his son,
"My son, do not attribute any partners to God:
attributing partners to Him is a terrible wrong."'[5]

I realize now that I do this form of psychological idolatry – knowingly or not – several times a day. No wonder the Prophet, peace and blessings upon him, said:

'What I fear most for my community is that they do things for other than the sake of Allah.'[6]

I've gained deep appreciation for this prayer of the Prophet, peace and blessings upon him:

'Allah, we seek refuge in You from associating partners with You knowingly; and we seek Your forgiveness from doing so unknowingly.'[7]

The moment we imagine that an object (a person, a career, a house) has the power to give or take away a feeling, we give that object far more importance than it's due in reality. We're preoccupied with it; we're pulled out of the present moment and we'd do anything to make it give us the feelings we want.

Our hearts are suddenly inflicted with all manner of diseases in relation to that object. We're inflicted with spiritual ailments – from greed, envy, and jealousy, to anger, hatred, and attachment. All because we imagine this 'thing' can cause our feelings, and so we imagine it has power over us. We become spiritually weak and materially attached.

The spiritual diseases of the heart from the Inside-Out

'Surely, in the breasts of humanity is a lump of flesh,
if sound then the whole body is sound,
and if corrupt then the whole body is corrupt.
Surely, it is the heart.'[8]

THE PROPHET MUHAMMAD, PEACE AND BLESSINGS UPON HIM

Some knowledge of the 24 'spiritual diseases of the heart,' and their cures, is an obligation on every individual Muslim. In the chapter on Remembrance I explained that scholars have specifically outlined these diseases and their spiritual cures. And I asserted that every one of them was based on a misunderstanding of the nature of thought, specifically where our feelings come from.

If we believe an object is causing our feelings, we become attached to the object and detached from Allah. This subtle form of idolatry causes needless psychological suffering, and unethical behaviors suddenly look like viable options. On the other hand, when we're aware that our feelings are always coming from Allah via the spiritual gift of thought, we're free from these 'diseases of the heart.'

There's insufficient space here to discuss all 24 diseases in depth – that would require another book. (As I mentioned earlier, the US scholar Shaykh Hamza Yusuf has done an excellent job of bringing to our attention the poem *Purification of the Heart* by Imam Mawlud.) However, I will share some insights into a few of them, to demonstrate the transcendence we find as we insightfully see the Inside-Out Reality.

Anger

'Strong is not the one who can win a fight;
strong is the one who can control their anger.'[9]

The Prophet Muhammad, peace and blessings upon him

A man once came to the Prophet, peace and blessings upon him, and said, 'Advise me.'

The Prophet replied, *'Do not become angry.'*

The man, who was perhaps looking for other advice, again asked, 'Advise me.'

The Prophet, peace and blessings upon him, replied, *'Do not become angry.'*

The third time, the man, who was perhaps becoming frustrated, said, 'Advise me!'

The Prophet, peace and blessings upon him, again replied, *'Do not become angry.'*

The Prophet, peace and blessings upon him, was very spiritually aware and astute. The advice he gave was for good reason. It must have been sobering for the man to hear that this was the only advice he needed from the final Messenger of Allah, peace and blessings upon him.

In a moment of anger, we can humiliate ourselves and do foolish things that we would never do in any other state, except perhaps drunkenness. For some, learning to let go of anger is the only thing that might save their most important relationships.

Among Muslim scholars, the jurists say that fulfilling the command 'Do not become angry' means 'Do not display anger toward others.' The spiritual masters take things to a deeper level and say that it means 'Do not even become angry.'

Transcending anger

The more I explore the Islamic tradition with an insightful understanding of the Inside-Out, the more it appears that the spiritual masters throughout the ages were also blessed with this understanding, even if they didn't articulate it in explicitly psychological terms. Here are the words of Imam Mawlud, in the poem *Purification of the Heart*, on the subject of anger:

> *'It has two treatments: one of them removes it altogether without trace. The other suppresses it should it manifest itself.'*

The poem states that there are two cures for anger: the first occurs before its onset and is to remind oneself of the emphasis in the Quran and Sunnah on forbearance and humility. In the text, the author makes an astute observation – that all of the prophets, peace and blessings upon them, were described as having these qualities.

Why would this cure remove anger altogether, without trace? I believe this is possible because, through these beautiful Quran verses and Prophetic stories, one hopes that Allah gifts the seeker with insights that automatically transform the way they look at the world.

When you know where your feelings are coming from, you've much less to be angry about. The path toward anger then crumbles by the power of insight. This is precisely why, when people come to our Paradigm Shift seminars, they tend to notice how much more 'chilled out' they are afterward. Things that would usually bother them no longer seem to have such an effect.

We spend the whole time exploring the One True Source of all human experience. Upon realizing that experience comes only from the spiritual power of thought, it's much harder to take our anger seriously.

The second cure for anger is given in this line from *Purification of the Heart*, which seems to be an acknowledgment of the Inside-Out Reality:

> *'Repel anger by perceiving at its onset that no one is doing anything, in reality, except the Almighty.'*

If we take 'no one is doing anything' to mean 'no one is causing your anger' (because angry feelings only come from angry thinking), then we have a precise description of how a mind trained in the Inside-Out Paradigm might react: angry feelings only come from angry thinking.

The poem then goes on to give the very wise Prophetic advice of making ritual ablution, remaining silent, sitting or lying down, and seeking refuge in Allah from the rejected Satan. Even if the person still experiences anger, these physical actions will keep them out of the trouble that results from misattributing the cause of their feelings to those around them.

Materialism

'*Dunya*' is a word that refers to this temporal, material world of 'things.' It's usually framed in contrast to the '*akhirah*,' or the eternal afterlife. The essential Islamic spiritual teaching is to have the '*dunya*' in your hand, but not in your heart. Love of this material world was considered by the spiritual master and scholar Ibn Ata'illah to be the root of all the other diseases of the heart. The Prophet, peace and blessings upon him, said:

'When love of the dunya *enters your heart,*
love of Allah leaves your heart.
When love of Allah enters your heart,
love of dunya *leaves your heart.'*[10]

On another occasion, he said:

> *'The life of this world compared to the hereafter is as if one of you were to put his finger in the ocean and take it out again, then compare the water that remains on his finger to the water that remains in the ocean.'*[11]

The Prophet, peace and blessings upon him, had little interest in the luxuries of this life because he knew – better than anyone – of the eternal rewards of the afterlife. The tribal leaders of his time offered him the delights of this world, if only he would stop sharing his message of the Oneness of Allah. They offered him all the wealth of the area and the most beautiful women, and offered to make him the head of all the tribes. His response was:

> *'By Allah, if they put the Sun in my right hand and the Moon in my left, on condition that I abandon this course, I would not abandon it until Allah has made me victorious, or I die trying.'*[12]

On another occasion, the Prophet's companion Umar, may Allah be pleased with him, saw that he was lying on a mat made of the leaves of date palms, with no bedding between him and the mat, and under his head was nothing but a leather pillow stuffed with the bark of the date tree. Umar said, 'My master, pray to Allah to grant prosperity to your followers.

He has given riches to the Romans and Persians, even though they are not believers.' The Prophet, peace and blessings upon him, replied:

*'O Umar – do you not prefer that they took the joys of this world [*dunya*], while we have the hereafter [*akhirah*]?'*[13]

It's important to note that while material *attachment* is considered a spiritual blemish, having things and gratefully enjoying them is allowed. Absolute asceticism is not the path of Islam. The prayer the Quran gives us is:

> 'Our Lord, give us the best of this life [dunya]
> and the best of the hereafter [akhirah].'[14]

However, some things are just more important than the delights of this world.

'The Prophet, peace and blessings upon him, said to one of his companions: "Shall I tell you of something worth more than a red camel?"

[At the time, a red camel was a valuable asset – perhaps the equivalent of a luxurious car today.]

'His companion said, "Of course!"

'The Prophet, peace and blessings upon him, replied, "To memorize a verse of the Quran."

'He then said, "Shall I tell what is more valuable than two red camels?"

'The companion affirmed. The Prophet, peace and blessings upon him, said, "To memorize two verses of the Quran."'[15]

Shaykh Zakariya, the Algerian scholar who narrated this story to me and inspired me to want to memorize the Quran, made an observation – how much less materialistic and deeply spiritual would people be if they viewed life in this way? How would our lives be different and be enhanced, if the point of life was not to gain as many material goods as possible, but rather to seek spiritual insight and sacred knowledge?

As Allah says in the Quran:

'The love of desirable things is made alluring for men –
women, children, gold and silver treasures piled up high,
horses with fine markings, livestock, and farmland –
these may be the joys of this life,
but Allah has the best place to return to.

'Say, "Would you like me to tell you of things that are better than all of these?" Their Lord will give those who are mindful of Allah, gardens graced with flowing streams, where they will stay with pure spouses and Allah's good pleasure. Allah is fully aware of His servants;

'Those who say, "our Lord, we believe, so forgive us our sins and protect us from suffering in the fire;"

'Those who are resilient, truthful, truly devoted,
who spend (for Allah), and pray before dawn for forgiveness.'[16]

Transcending materialism

All of this raises some questions. 'How much materialism is *too* much?' 'How much money is too much?' 'Where do we draw the line between receive "the best" of this world and being materialistic?' From the Inside-Out, the answer becomes clear and obvious.

My niece, who was 15 at the time, once came to visit me in London for a weekend. I happened to have a Paradigm Shift training course running, so she had to come along. By the end of the weekend, after sharing some of what is contained in this book, but with a much more in-depth exploration of the Inside-Out, I asked her what she made of it. When I heard her analysis, it stopped me in my tracks.

Usually at these events, a lot of people are deeply impacted, while others hear something that they know is true, but the penny hasn't quite dropped for them yet. From my niece's response, it was clear which category she fell into. From this perspective there's no need for a clear line.

My niece said: 'Before I came to this training, I thought to myself, *a new iPhone "shouldn't" make me happy because that would be materialistic*. (She had an old phone with a cracked screen.)

But now I can see that a brand new iPhone *actually can't* make me happy because that's just not how feelings work.'

I was beyond proud, *masha'Allah.* May Allah continue to bless her with light, insight, and guidance, along with her sisters and cousins.

'Detach yourself from this world, and Allah will love you.
Detach yourself from what people possess
and the people will love you.'[17]

THE PROPHET MUHAMMAD, PEACE AND BLESSINGS UPON HIM

Self-righteousness

As we're nearing the end of this book, I want to share with you what has been, in my experience, one of the most insidious expressions of the diseases of the heart. Those who consider themselves 'religious' or 'spiritual' are particularly susceptible to it. As we continue on our spiritual journey, we need to keep these teachings close to heart.

Self-righteousness is an amalgamation of several diseases, particularly arrogance, showing off, and being judgmental. Its external expression is being judgmental toward others and its internal reflection is taking praise and blame personally.

This disease of 'self-righteousness' has nothing to do with actual righteousness with Allah. It's to consider ourselves morally, spiritually, or religiously superior to our sisters and brothers in humanity. And hence to consider others inferior to us.

Arrogance

The Prophet, peace and blessings upon him, said:

> *'No one who has an atom's weight of arrogance in his heart will enter Paradise.'*
>
> *'Someone said, "But a man loves to have beautiful clothes and shoes."*
>
> *'The Prophet, peace and blessings upon him, said: "Allah is beautiful and loves beauty. Arrogance means denying rights and looking down on people."'*[18]

In many cultures, people who are devoted to their religion are disliked. This isn't because others dislike their prayers, or their attempts to be closer to Allah. It's because of the flawed character traits they display, which the spiritual teachings they follow aim to purify them from.

Among these is arrogance (*kibr*), which is part and parcel of looking down on those who appear to be less pious or righteous. Arrogance can be about anything, such as wealth or power. It's one of the most dangerous sins of the heart, and is a quality of 'those in denial' in the Quran, including the Pharaoh of Egypt and Satan, the rejected.

The Quran, making this connection, says:

> 'I will divert my signs from those who show arrogance without right.'[19]

> 'Allah seals the heart of every arrogant tyrant.'[20]

> 'Allah does not love the arrogant.'[21]

I used to think of arrogance in terms of morality. I figured that we all sin, myself included, so I guess I can't look down on others who sin. However, in my mind, I was only thinking about externally visible sins, not the internal state of the hearts that do them. This approach led me to become judgmental, even though I really disliked that quality in others.

Let's assume that you and I are Muslims, and that we both think praying five times a day is an excellent idea, and that not doing so is 'sinful.' If I manage the external action of prayer one day, and you don't, I now have something to be arrogant about. I judge myself as being better, and you as being worse.

If sinning is our reason for not being arrogant as we progress on the spiritual path, what happens when we sin less? It can lead us to become very arrogant, thinking we're better than those who are not as religious as us. Or, it could unconsciously make us more inclined toward continuing to sin, out of a secret desire to not be arrogant. The Prophet, peace and blessings upon him, said:

'Allah does not look at your outward appearance or image,
But looks into your hearts and at your intentions.'[22]

Transcending arrogance

The nature of the Inside-Out is such that sometimes we see it and are aware of it, and sometimes we don't. It doesn't seem to matter how evolved we are. No one seems to ever get to the point where they never go 'Outside-In.' It seems as though Allah built this into the system. This is what keeps us humble.

When I started looking at things from an Inside-Out perspective, rather than an externally moral perspective, I noticed that I was rapidly running out of reasons to be arrogant. This is because of the realization that every disease of the heart comes from the same Outside-In misunderstanding, which I fall for myself every day.

We can fall for this misunderstanding at any moment, even if we're externally impeccable. The fact that the worst thing anyone else ever does is out of the same misunderstanding that I can (and do!) fall into at any given moment, engenders humility and compassion rather than arrogance and showing off.

Every time we realize we were falling for the Outside-In Illusion, we're being kept humble. At every turn, we're reminded of this: the moment we find ourselves to be humble, the arrogance of the Outside-In Illusion has already entered.

Showing off

'I do not fear that you will worship the Sun, the stars, and the Moon, but I fear your worshipping other than Allah by showing off.'[23]

The Prophet Muhammad, peace and blessings upon him

'My greatest fear for you is the lesser idolatry: It is showing off. Allah Almighty will say to them on the Day of Recompense, when people are being recompensed for their deeds: "Go to those for whom you made a show in the world and look, do you find any reward with them?"'[24]

The Prophet Muhammad, peace and blessings upon him

The second element of self-righteousness is showing off, particularly in acts of worship, piety, or knowledge. This is to perform an act of worship or goodness in order to be seen by the creation, instead of for the sake of the Creator. It's the opposite of sincerity.

The spiritual master Ibn Ata'illah said: 'Actions are but erected empty forms and their soul is the presence of the secret of sincerity in them.' Showing off, or ostentation, is based on desiring the praise of others, which is inextricably bound up with fearing the negative opinion of others. In our world of social media, this trap is closer than ever.

Transcending showing off

All of these are expressions of the Outside-In Illusion. In reality, the feelings we think the praise will give us can only come from Allah, and only via thought. It's the same with the negative feelings we think others' negative opinions of us will have. Taking things personally in this way is also classed as a 'disease of the heart.'

Transcending this comes from a deep understanding of the Inside-Out Reality, which is pointed to in this Prophetic saying:

'Be mindful of Allah, and He will take care of you.
Be mindful of Allah, and you shall find Him at your side.

'If you ask, ask of Allah.
If you seek help, seek help from Allah.

'Know that if the whole world were to gather together to benefit you,
they would not be able to benefit you,
except with that which Allah had already prescribed for you.

'And if the whole world were to gather together to harm you,
they would not be able to harm you,
except with that which Allah had already prescribed for you.

'The pens have been lifted, and the pages are dry.'[25]

Being judgmental

The third element of self-righteousness is being judgmental of others. This is clearly linked with the other two elements.

It's the antithesis of the essential attribute of the believer: to have a high opinion of others, and of Allah. Being judgmental is a sickness that destroys religious communities from within.

In case it was not already crystal clear from the chapter on 'Denial,' it's completely *haram* (forbidden) to damn anyone to Hell, or to claim knowledge that someone will go to Hell. There is only One True Judge: Allah. Anyone else is trying to usurp Allah's power.

In fact, there's a tradition that on the Day of Judgment, the one who damns another to Hell will see that person absolved of their sins and be thrown into Hell themselves. The Prophet, peace and blessings upon him, said:

> '*No one accuses another of being a sinner or a* 'kafir' *[one in denial], but it reflects back on him if the other is not.*'[26]

Our aim, instead, is to overlook faults, in the hope that Allah will overlook our faults, and to always have the highest opinion of others, in the hope that Allah raises our spiritual station. Hamdun al-Qassar, one of the great early Muslims, said: 'If one of your friends errs, make 70 excuses for them. If your heart is unable to do this, then know that the shortcoming is in your own self.' One of my teachers told us: 'Even if you see a man with wine dripping from his beard… assume someone threw it in his face.'

As the Quran puts it:

'Dear Believers, Avoid suspicions,
for many suspicions are sinful.'[27]

Transcending being judgmental

Once again, the Inside-Out underlines this. The moment we find ourselves being judgmental toward other people, it's obvious that we've fallen for the Outside-In Illusion. The moment there's a sense of superiority, or a self-righteous feeling of 'I'm right, you're wrong,' we've lost the clarity of the Inside-Out. We might not yet see how, but we know that we have, and that arrogance has entered.

The reason we're argumentative is that we want the feeling of being right, and think this feeling means that we *are* right. This isn't true – it just means that we're being self-righteous. There is a difference. When we're Inside-Out and clearly see that our feelings can only come from our own thinking, we're aligned with Truth and we don't need to convince anyone else of our stance.

Imam Shafi'i said: 'I have never spoken to anyone without wishing that Allah, the Most High, would grant him success, guidance, support, care and protection. And I have never spoken with anyone while caring whether the Allah clarified the truth through my words or theirs.'[28]

Perhaps the most beautiful thing about the Inside-Out understanding is that there's one thing to be deeply aware of, and infinite things that may be insightfully realized through this one understanding. We don't necessarily need to memorize all the diseases of the heart and their cures (although, may Allah give those of us who wish to the *tawfiq* – divine success – to do so). We do, however, absolutely need to understand deeply that the only Source of our experience is the divine gift of thought in the moment.

I may sound like a broken record here, repeating this statement perhaps hundreds of times throughout this book. However, losing sight of the One True Source of our moment-to-moment experience leads to 'psychological idolatry,' and ultimately to all of the spiritual diseases of the heart. Since we as human beings will always repeat our mistakes, the solution bears repeating:

> *'The sicknesses of the mind are feelings that we create and put onto objects. All mental illness comes from putting our feelings onto objects. But if you can see the objects without the feelings, you are healthy.'*
>
> **Sydney Banks**

CHAPTER 17

Forgiveness – the Self-Healing System

'Allah the Almighty said:

O son of Adam, so long as you call upon Me and ask of Me,
I shall forgive you for what you have done,
and I shall not mind.

O son of Adam, were your sins to reach the clouds of the sky
and were you then to ask forgiveness of Me,
I would forgive you.

O son of Adam, were you to come to Me with sins
nearly as great as the Earth,
and were you then to face Me, ascribing no partner to Me,
I would bring you forgiveness nearly as great as the Earth.'[1]

THE PROPHET MUHAMMAD,
PEACE AND BLESSINGS UPON HIM

After looking at what it means to be in denial and to fall into psychological idolatry, and after exploring a few of the diseases of the heart, this chapter now allows us to breathe a sigh of relief. No book on the Soul of Islam could possibly be complete without addressing the first and most critical step in our spiritual development: forgiveness.

The Prophet Muhammad, peace and blessings upon him, said:

'I swear by Him in whose hand is my soul,
if you were a people who did not commit sin,
Allah would take you away and replace you
with a people who would sin,
and then seek Allah's forgiveness, so He could forgive them.'[2]

Falling off the Straight Path

It's a given that we'll fall short of the mark of excellence that Islam has set for us. As much as we may aim to do good actions, speak only Truth, be kind to everyone, be resilient on following the Straight Path, not be in denial of Truth, struggle to do what's right – even when it's the hardest thing to do – and live into all of the values of Islam, we will all, inevitably, fail. We all make mistakes.

Allah, the Most Forgiving, loves to forgive. The more we come to terms with this reality, the easier it is for us to be overwhelmed with awe at the generosity of the Most Forgiving.

Forgiveness is the process of self-acceptance and healing. Rather than never falling off the path, our objective is to fall, but get back up as quickly as we fell down, and before we move on, seek forgiveness.

What is a 'sin,' anyway?

Rather than explore the objective morality put forth by the religion of Islam – which, again, falls under the 'body' of Islam and may not make much sense to non-Muslims – let's keep this simple and universal. A sin, in essence, is anything we say or do that harms ourselves or others. Plainly put: mistakes, errors, ego-driven harmful behavior, or all-out evil actions.

The underlying message of the Quran is Absolute Divine Unity, or '*tawhid*,' but in the Quran we find a constant dynamic tension between opposing forces. As much as there are 'believers' (in Truth), there are those 'in denial' of Truth; as much as there are 'good actions,' there are 'evil actions'; as much as there is Heaven, there is Hell; as much as there is gratitude, there is ingratitude; and just as there is a temporary, worldly life, so is there an eternal afterlife.

Muslims don't believe in a 'Good God' that only does 'good things.' Rather, we believe in the Transcendent Allah Who is beyond time, space, and matter, and limited human conceptions of morality. Allah the Transcendent is the Source of all creation and He inspires us to do good and gain eternal reward; He gives us the ability to use our free will to do evil.

There's a general consensus among humanity that certain traits and characteristics are not good for us, or those around us, and that certain clearly harmful behaviors are immoral. The consequences of these behaviors, Islam teaches us, harm the one who commits them, first and foremost.

We all sin. We all sometimes fall into denial of Truth. We all go Outside-In, and believe in the impossible. We all sometimes use our imagination to give power to objects that in reality have no power.

We can all become arrogant, ignorant, and self-righteous, sometimes. We've all lived into the noble virtues of Islam, and we've all missed the mark and messed up plenty of times too. And we all continue to do all of this on a daily basis. May Allah have mercy on us, forgive us, and protect us from needless psychological suffering and the harm it brings. The Prophet Muhammad, peace and blessings upon him, made this beautifully reassuring statement:

'Satan, the rejected, said to Allah:
"I shall misguide your servants for as long as
their souls are in their bodies."
'Allah replied: "Then I shall forgive them for as long as
they turn to Me in repentance."'[3]

Between blame and forgiveness

Through this dynamic tension in the Quran, the Transcendent One leaves us, as always, with two options. We can blame, or we can forgive. We can blame others and hold grudges, or we can forgive them and let go. We can blame ourselves and indulge in self-depreciating guilt trips, or we can forgive ourselves and move on. We can stumble around in the darkness, or we can wake up and take hopeful steps toward the light.

Forgiveness is a fascinating process of introspection that makes us seek the balance between two extremes: 'I didn't do anything wrong' and 'I did something so wrong, it can't be forgiven.' Whether we forgive ourselves, or others, or seek the forgiveness of Allah, the result is always the same: we experience deep inner healing.

'Be merciful to others, and Allah will be merciful to you;
be forgiving to others, and Allah will forgive you.'[4]

THE PROPHET MUHAMMAD, PEACE AND BLESSINGS UPON HIM

The way we are with creation is the way the Creator is with us. And we're part of creation. Forgive yourself as much as you want Allah's forgiveness.

Sin from the Inside-Out

This beautiful metaphor to describe the Islamic approach to sin can be found in the works of the mystic al-Ghazali and the poet Rumi.

In the same way that we wouldn't look down on someone who has fallen physically ill, we couldn't possibly look down on someone who has fallen spiritually ill. The heart of the sinner has been afflicted with a sickness, which manifests itself in their engaging in destructive behavior. The attitude of the spiritually aware believers is to be grateful to Allah that we don't have that particular affliction, and to sincerely pray that they too are healed from it.

It's highly unlikely that we would 'hate' or blame someone because they have cancer. And yet it's easy to hate and blame someone who engages in immoral actions (especially ones that affect us). This is only because of our lack of perception of the spiritual reality: they've fallen into the Outside-In Illusion, as we all often do. We are them, and they are us.

The man destined for paradise

There are so many beautiful little anecdotes and sayings of the Prophet, peace and blessings upon him, about forgiveness. To inspire us all to know the magnitude of the virtue of forgiveness, here is one of my favorites.

The Prophet, peace and blessings upon him, was once sitting in the mosque with a few of his companions, and he said to them: *'A man will now enter, from among the people of Paradise.'*[5]

An unsuspecting man then walked in. This happened on two other occasions, and the same man walked in. One of the Prophet's companions, Abdullah, may Allah be pleased with him, wanted to find out what was so special about this man. So he did some detective work.

He made up an excuse and asked the man if he could stay over at his house for three days. In the Arab Bedouin culture of the time it was customary to let anyone be a guest for up to the three days, so the man politely accepted.

Abdullah noted that the man didn't do anything out of the ordinary: he didn't fast all the time, or more than the other companions. He slept some of the night and did a little extra prayer before the pre-dawn prayer, but this was also common for the companions, may Allah be pleased with them. So, after the three days, Abdullah told the man why he'd requested to stay with him, and asked him what could be the reason he was 'from the people of Paradise.'

The man, may Allah be pleased with him, was overwhelmed with joy to hear the news that the Prophet, peace and blessings upon him, had said this about him. However, he sincerely couldn't think of anything that would isolate him from the other blessed companions. After some reflection, he said that there was just one thing that occurred to him. 'Every night before I go to sleep,' he said, 'I forgive whoever has wronged me. I remove any bad feelings toward anyone from my heart.'

This is the essence of Islamic spirituality. This is the Soul of Islam.

Forgiveness from the Inside-Out

When we realize that no one has ever caused our hurt feelings, what is there to forgive? It's true that others may have acted in a way that we think of as immoral, or actually harmful. It's also true that this is only ever because of their falling into the same Outside-In misunderstanding that we've fallen into.

I once had a student who was very upset that someone she knew had abused someone she loved. She was overcome with anger toward the man, and had held onto it for years. She'd become frustrated that other students on the course would talk to her about 'forgiveness.'

'How could I possibly forgive him?! He doesn't deserve forgiveness!' she cried. *Yes*, I told her, *but you do*. Her grudge didn't harm him – it was harming her. And her forgiveness would only benefit her.

After an in-depth session, she eventually came to realize that the man's abuse was immoral, but it was not the source of her anger. And those around her who seemed less angry were not less moral than her. She realized that her anger was coming from the way she was thinking about the situation, not the situation itself – as terrible as it was.

All this time, she'd been holding the man responsible, not just for his crime but for her *feelings* about his crime. The moment she let go of this misunderstanding, the space for insight, and eventually compassion, opened up.

With insight, she eventually came to see that she'd been Outside-In – attributing her anger to this man's terrible actions. At some point it occurred to her that before he could possibly have engaged in abusive behavior, he had to have been completely deluded by the Outside-In – just as she was.

The moment she saw this, she was overwhelmed with empathy for him. In this moment she saw his psychological innocence. A heavy weight was removed from her mind, and her heart was clear again. She experienced the healing power of forgiveness; this is what there is to forgive.

Guilt-ridden saints and happy sinners

During a different coaching session, a client told me she felt overwhelmed with guilt about something she'd done. It was clear to me that she hadn't actually done anything wrong, from an Islamic or a universal moral perspective, but pointing this out didn't help alleviate the guilt.

She'd decided not to move forward on a project, leaving a friend disappointed in her. However, she wasn't breaking an agreement or a contract: she'd simply changed her mind. I asked her, out of curiosity: 'What do you think your feelings of guilt are telling you?'

She replied: 'They're telling me that she could be right – maybe I'm being a bad person.'

'Okay, what else are they telling you?' I asked.

She went on, 'They're telling me that Allah is going to punish me on the Day of Judgment for not moving forward with this project.'

By now I could tell my client was on the verge of seeing something amazing about Allah and life. I asked her one more time: 'What else are they telling you?'

She replied, 'Maybe the guilt is telling me I should just ignore my intuition and continue working with her.'

At this point, we both knew she was talking nonsense. I finally interjected: 'None of those responses is true. Your guilt isn't telling you anything about Allah's opinion of you, or the project, or who is right or wrong. In fact, your guilt doesn't even know you have a project or a business! The only thing that feeling of guilt is telling you, is that you're thinking in a guilty way.' She immediately smiled because she knew I was speaking truth, but she hadn't quite wrapped her head around it.

Most people think that a feeling of guilt means we've sinned. This is not true. And it's not logical. If guilt is a measure of how much we've sinned, the measure must be completely broken. There are millions of people who sin, and who feel no guilt or remorse (myself included). And there are many people who don't sin, as was the case with this client, but who feel terrible levels of guilt (myself included).

The idea that feeling guilty means that Allah will punish us is equally untrue. We've absolutely no idea whether Allah has completely forgiven us or will punish us, regardless of how we feel. We might feel terribly guilty but have already been completely forgiven; or we might feel absolutely fine about a crime that was, from a divine perspective, not acceptable or forgiven.

The moment we start believing that something other than thought in the moment is the source of feeling, is the moment we stop being principled, paradigmatic, and precise in our understanding of how Allah made our psychology work. If anything, guilt is merely a feeling that's kicked in to remind you that in that moment, you're no longer seeing life clearly, and that perhaps it's not wise to trust the way you're thinking about things right now.

Guilt doesn't tell us how much we've sinned. Guilt tells us that we've lost sight of the truth of how immensely forgiving Allah, the Most Forgiving, truly is.

Forgiveness – the process of self-correction

'The Lord descends every night to the lowest heaven
when one-third of the night remains and says:

"Who will call upon Me, that I may answer him?
Who will ask of Me, that I may give him?
Who will seek My forgiveness, that I may forgive him?"'[6]

THE PROPHET MUHAMMAD, PEACE AND BLESSINGS UPON HIM

'If there was a river at the door of anyone of you
and he took a bath in it five times a day,
would you notice any dirt on him?'

'They said, "Not a trace of dirt would be left."
The Prophet, peace and blessings upon him added:
"That is the example of the five prayers,
with which Allah erases sins."'[7]

The Prophet Muhammad, peace and blessings upon him

The following process of forgiveness is a description of what we do automatically when we realize the truth of the Inside-Out in the context of a situation we've been Outside-In about.

To seek forgiveness, we must first recognize that we were in error. This happens automatically the moment we wake up from the illusion of thinking, and acting, as though another person, thing, or situation was the cause of our feelings. Operating from this illusion, harsh words and harmful, even foolish, actions make sense to us.

When we transcend this illusion, and realize that our feelings were caused by our own thinking all along, we suddenly realize just how much in error we've been. Next, we see that the enormity of the mistakes we made while we were deluded by the Outside-In are minuscule in comparison with the vastness of the forgiveness of the All-Forgiving.

To think that we've done something so great that it can't be forgiven, or that we're not worth forgiveness, is to underestimate ourselves and the Greatness of Allah, the Most Forgiving. That underestimation would be a true sin, and moreover, illogical.

Having had this insightful change of heart, from a place of realization, a Muslim will naturally say the Prophetic formula '*astaghfirullah*' – 'I seek Allah's forgiveness.' It no longer makes sense for us to carry on as we were, so we transform. Simply put, the process of forgiveness is the process of insightful self-correction.

How to seek Allah's forgiveness

Here are some beautiful Prophetic prayers that we can recite as we go through this process of seeking Allah's forgiveness:

'Allah, You are the Forgiver. You love to forgive. So forgive me.'[8]

'Allah, You are my Lord, there is no deity except You.
You created me and I am Your servant.
And, I broke my covenant and promise to You.
I seek refuge in You from the evil I have done.
I recognize the blessings You have given me
and I recognize my mistake.
So forgive me. For indeed, no one can forgive sins, except You.'[9]

Who is to judge?

A man once came to the Prophet, peace and blessings upon him, and asked: 'Who will be the Judge, on the Day of Judgment?'

The Prophet, peace and blessings upon him, immediately answered, *'Allah.'*

The man responded, 'Allah Himself?!'

I imagine the Prophet, peace and blessings upon him, was taken aback at this very basic question with a crystal-clear answer. He replied, *'Yes, Allah Himself.'*

The man laughed, and started walking away. Before the man left, the Prophet, peace and blessings upon him, asked him: *'Why did you laugh?'*

He replied: 'Indeed the Most Generous will be very generous in His account, and when he takes into account our sins, then surely He (the Most Forgiving), will overlook them.'

The Prophet, peace and blessings upon him, confirmed. The man then smiled with delight and walked away.

The Prophet, peace and blessings upon him, said to the others, *'Certainly this man has understood.'*[10]

Allah the Most Generous, the Most Lovingly Kind, the Most Forgiving, is the only One who will ultimately judge us. All of the descriptions of Allah in the Quran ought to give us great hope and inspiration to continue to be devoted to Him and in service to humanity, by embodying these qualities in ourselves.

Relying on love

'Your despair at falling off the Straight Path is an indication that you were relying too heavily on your actions.'[11]

Ibn Ata'illah

I was completely astonished when I first read this extract from the *Aphorisms*, a text by the spiritual master Ibn Ata'illah. It was the first time after discovering the Inside-Out Paradigm that I'd read anything by a Muslim that struck me as having been written from a completely Inside-Out perspective.

This is when I realized that there had indeed been enlightened people throughout the ages who lived, taught, and wrote from the Inside-Out, even though they didn't use this psychological vocabulary to describe it. As I continued reading, it just got better and better.

The idea that we would fall into despair because we sinned means that we're operating as though our good actions would be enough to get us into Heaven. From an Islamic perspective, this is a misunderstanding of how life works. The Prophet, peace and blessings upon him, corrected this misunderstanding, saying:

> *'No one will get into Heaven because of their good actions.'*
>
> *'The companions asked: "Not even you, O Messenger of Allah?"*
>
> *'Not even me, were it not for Allah's Loving Kindness enveloping me.'*[12]

And so, in the end, we're returned to the starting point: loving kindness.

CONCLUSION

The Healing Power of Islam

'Allah will not change the state of a people,
until they change, within themselves.'[1]

QURAN

This is the Islam we believe in. This is the Islam we believed in before the 'goodness' or 'peacefulness' of the religion was called into question. And this is the Islam we will continue to believe in, long after the insanity of terrorism has faded away.

However, until that time, because of the frequency of terrorism and the level of destruction and havoc it causes, it seems appropriate to share some thoughts on how we might overcome this challenge, together.

How to heal after a terrorist attack

Within two weeks of my completing the first draft of this book, two terrorist attacks took place in the two cities I consider home: Manchester and London. One targeted a concert and the other is occurring in London as I write this. I can literally hear the sirens outside.

The first attack was in Manchester, at an Ariana Grande concert. My nieces are fans of the US pop star, so when the first news reports came up on my phone, I immediately texted the eldest, who had just turned 16. I didn't get a response. After a night spent worrying about the two girls, praying and convincing myself of how unlikely it was that they had been caught up in the attack, I awoke to discover what had happened. I saw that one of my nieces had 'liked' a post my brother had made on Facebook, giving condolences to the innocent who had lost their lives.

Later that morning, my niece texted me, telling me that everyone was okay and apologizing that her phone didn't have internet access (I'll never understand how a whole generation can be on their phones virtually all the time, yet never answer texts when you need them to!) The relief was bittersweet because something occurred to me: I was happy that my nieces were okay, but I knew that other people's nieces were not. So many young girls and women were out that night, enjoying some entertainment – just as my nieces could have been.

I then recognized the hypocrisy in myself. I claim that all lives are equal, and yet I felt relief, not despair, on discovering that it was not my nieces, but someone else's, who had been harmed. A few years earlier, when their mother (my sister

Sonia) tragically passed away, one meaning of this verse of the Quran become apparent to me:

> 'If anyone kills an (innocent) person,
> it is as if he kills all of mankind,
> while if he saves a life,
> it is as if he saves the lives of all mankind.'[2]

It occurred to me that the reason it's like 'killing all of mankind' is because there's someone out there who loves that person so much – they have lost their beloved – the murderer might as well have killed all of mankind.

In the chapter on Resilience I shared that the following verses of the Quran were of great consolation to me when I lost my sister. I've included them again here in the hope that they can be a source of benefit and light to all the victims and survivors of terrorism, and their families, who bravely carry on, day after day. You are our inspiration. And you live these teachings in ways that give the rest of us hope:

> 'Dear Believers, seek help through patience and prayer.
> Indeed, Allah is with the patient.
> And do not say about those who are killed in the way of Allah,
> "They are dead." Rather, they are alive, but you perceive it not.
> And We will surely test you with something of fear and hunger

> and a loss of wealth and lives and fruits,
> but give good tidings to the resilient.
> Those who, when disaster strikes them, say,
> "To Allah we belong, and to Him is our return."
> Those are the ones upon whom are blessings and mercy from their Lord.
> And it is they who are truly guided.'[3]
>
> QURAN

May the mercy, blessings, and beautiful guidance of the Most Merciful, Most Wise, descend upon you, my friend; may you always be protected from any harm, and may your status be raised in this life and eternally.

How we can permanently end terrorism

When I'm invited to speak on TV news programs in the aftermath of a terrorist attack – which seem to be occurring all too often these days – I want to say something that I don't know how to articulate in a soundbite.

And I don't know how to say it without sounding crazy to an audience who, by and large, were brought up with a material worldview and haven't been trained in spiritual teachings. There's only one way that I can see to end terrorism. I say this to everyone, of every faith and none:

If you want to stop terrorism,
don't be a terrorist.

Don't terrorize yourself inside of your own mind. Don't inflict terror on your family or friends – with terrible thoughts, words, and deeds – because of your emotional state in the moment. Don't fall into the same trap that terrorists fall into. What you do and how you think and live may seem unconnected to the violent actions of a few hateful people, but I assure you, it is not.

Terrorism is a physical manifestation of the spiritual disease that has infected the collective consciousness of humanity. If you want to raise the collective consciousness of humanity, raise your own level of consciousness. If you want to heal all of the world, heal all of yourself. If you want to create peace in all of the world, create peace in all of yourself. If you want the world to be a more loving place, be a more loving person.

This is the spiritual path. This is the spiritual teaching of every enlightened woman and man who has ever walked the face of the Earth. And, as lovely as it sounds, we throw this spiritual truth out the moment we get scared, angry, or hateful.

Our ego kicks in and says: 'They're bombing us and yet you want us to be "understanding" and "peaceful," and "spiritual"?!' My answer is: 'Yes – that's exactly what I want for us. I believe that's exactly what every founder of every religion, and the One Source of all religion, wants for us.

Of course, the military and security forces of each country will do their jobs to the best of their ability to keep us safe. However, most of us are not in the military. There's literally nothing we can do to physically stop a terrorist attack.

We find out about them only once it's too late. Our attempts to destroy the areas of the world in which we think the terrorists originated have failed, time and again. Killing innocent people as a reaction to innocent people being killed is a bit like trying to put out a fire by pouring oil over it.

What each of us can do

There is, however, something that we can *all* do to eliminate the root of all terrorism. The root of all terrorism is the Outside-In Illusion. Terrorists have completely fallen prey to the illusion that the hatred, anger, and fear that we feel is coming from someone 'out there,' and not our own minds 'in here.'

Our feelings – positive or negative – don't come from the state of the world around us, but from the state of the world inside us. The moment we imagine that our feelings come from other people – however immoral their actions may be – is the moment we fall into the mindset of terrorism.

If these attacks continue in the way they have been, I honestly don't know how much more Western countries can take before they completely turn on their Muslim communities – in much the same way they did to the Jewish community not so long ago. In the USA there have been calls for internment camps for Muslims. In Australia, there was a call for any Muslims who believe in the *Shariah* to be banned from the country. (As you learnt earlier, all Muslims believe in the *Shariah*, by definition). If anything, it seems more justifiable now to hate Muslims than it was to hate Jews back in the early twentieth century.

However, this bigotry and hatred comes from exactly the same place, and leads to exactly the same consequences as the terrorists' hatred of us Westerners. We have to be better than that. We have to take the spiritual path because it's the path of truth, peace, and transcendence. It enhances our lives, brings peace to our minds, and makes the world a better place.

The Prophet, peace and blessings upon him, taught us that humanity is one body. When one part of the body gets sick, the whole body reacts with fever. It's as if you're one cell in the living organism called 'humanity.' When one part of an ecosystem becomes sick, it affects the whole body. When one part of an ecosystem becomes more healthy, that too affects the whole body.

Your psychological, spiritual sickness affects the entire body of humanity. Your mental health and wellbeing is essential to the wellbeing of humanity. Your primary responsibility is to keep yourself healthy. Put on your own oxygen mask before trying to help those sitting next to you. Be the one who keeps their head while all around are losing theirs. Be the calm that weathers the storms.

Feed your soul. Strengthen it. Nurture it. Nourish it with divine wisdom and abundant gratitude. Cherish your own soul as if all of humanity depends on it, because your soul is worth the whole of humanity. Your soul *is* the soul of humanity.

Realize who you truly are. Now that you've been touched by these teachings, you might be aware of something that has, in reality, been true all along.

You are the Soul of Islam

This book contains the essential teachings of our religion – the Soul of Islam. And, as you embrace the spiritual values contained in this book, you become part of the Soul of Islam.

- It happens every time you show loving kindness to creation and receive the *Loving Kindness* of the divine.
- It happens every time you attempt to deepen your *knowledge* of Allah, and are continually transformed with the gift of divine insight.
- It happens every time you spread the greeting of *'Peace'* with a smile.
- It happens every time you inculcate intense *presence* and enter Allah's Presence, as illusory thoughts of past and future drop away.
- It happens every time you *remember Allah*, in secret, or declare His Greatness from the top of a minaret.
- It happens every time you *speak the truth*, despite your fears, and your affairs are straightened out by the One who gave them to you.

- It happens every time you show *resilience* in the face of adversity, knowing that Allah is with the resilient.
- It happens every time you *take inspired, imperfect action* to benefit those around you, knowing the spiritual reality that through service, you're benefiting more than them.
- It happens every time you pause for long enough to be overwhelmed by the beauty of the world and feel *abundant gratitude* for it.
- It happens every time you *continue to struggle*, and fight the good fight, knowing that the reward is in the effort and the results are with Allah.
- It happens every time you *transcend denial*, accept truth, and save yourself and those around you from the harm of your own misunderstanding.
- It happens every time you let go of the illusion and so are purified and *spiritually transformed*.
- It happens every single time you drop guilt by remembering that the worst thing you've ever done is minuscule in comparison with the magnitude of *the All-Forgiving*.

Where do we go from here?

After reading this book, I imagine that some readers may be almost shocked by how dramatically different the true teachings of Islam are, compared with the image that's been presented to them. This book contains the spiritual values of Islam – the essence of the whole religion. In a way, this is my best effort at articulating why I'm a Muslim, and what I wish everyone could know about the beauty of our faith. You now have a deeper understanding of the true religion of Islam than most English-speaking people in the world. The question is: where do we go from here? I have three suggestions.

1. Deepen your knowledge

I've prepared some resources that may benefit you if you want to deepen your knowledge of Islam, and the Inside-Out Paradigm. Visit our website – www.InsideTheSoulOfIslam .com/Guide – to access all of what follows:

- An accompanying video guide to give you more insight into the teachings in this book.
- A list of reliable, authoritative Muslim scholars and/or institutions. The limitations of trying to create a list of competent scholars are many, not least of which is the fact that I don't know all of the Muslim scholars in the world (as I said earlier, I'm at present a competent student of Islam but not a scholar.) However, I've listed some of my favorite teachers of sacred knowledge.
- A list of highly recommended books on the mind, body, and soul of Islam, as well as comprehensive introductions to the religion. I've included books and courses on the

Prophet's life, peace and blessings upon him, and my favorite translations of the Quran.

- A free, in-depth online masterclass that provides a comprehensive overview of the Inside-Out Paradigm, along with resources and courses to help deepen your understanding of it.

2. Spread the message

I've always wanted a good, comprehensive introduction to Islam that shares the beauty of its life-enhancing spiritual wisdom. This book is my attempt.

The vast majority of people in the West have no idea about the essential teachings of Islam of which you're now aware. Share what you've learnt with others. Study it. Teach it. Use it to create seminars and courses.

If you're a Muslim, make sure your mosque and public prayer spaces have plenty of copies of this book available. Gift them to your work colleagues and neighbors. Create study circles based on the teachings in this book, and open them up to the public. If you're a Christian and hold Bible studies, or if you're from any faith and your community is open to exploring other religions, feel free to use this text as a starting point.

3. Join our community

In reality, Islam can't be learnt from a book. It must be absorbed from the inheritors of the Prophet, peace and blessings upon him. I would love to introduce you to these gems, and pray that you're blessed to meet them. To facilitate that, being part of our community is the best next step.

It's a rare and beautiful thing to find fellow spiritual seekers on the path to a deeper understanding of Allah. The key to holding firm on any spiritual path is to find others whose mere presence reminds you of Allah, and who speak words of truth and love.

I hope we'll find some fellow wayfarers in our global community of Inside-Out Spiritual Seekers, which is growing. You can find us by signing up on the website, where I'll direct you to our latest online and in-person meetings. I'll also keep you updated on our latest 'Inside the Soul Of Islam' and 'Paradigm Shift' live seminars.

A final thought

The spiritual master Ibn Ata'illah said:

> *'The value of spiritual work is commensurate to the hearts that perform them. No spiritual work proves trivial if it appears from a heart detached to this life. No spiritual work proves plentiful if it appears from a heart attached to this life.'*[4]

Time is of the essence, as our journey through this life in this world is short. As al-Ghazali said:

'Live as long as you may, but know that one day you will die.

Love whomsoever you wish, but know that one day you will taste separation.

Do whatever you want, but know that one day, you will be held accountable.'[5]

In reality, we may, or may not, ever get to meet each other in person. Either way, pray for me, as I pray for all readers of this book.

May Allah bless this book, accept it, and bestow light, guidance, and true spiritual insight upon all of its readers, from now until the end of time. May each chapter, page, paragraph, and sentence be filled with truth, wisdom, and uplifting insight that touches the heart of every reader.

And may the peace, love, and blessings of Allah be showered upon our master and teacher Muhammad, the messenger and servant of Allah, and upon all those who follow his Path of Peace and greatness, from now until the end of time.

And may the Peace, Love, and Blessings of Allah be with you, always.

References

Note: The 'Quran' entries below refer to the Holy Quran chapter number and verse number, while the 'Collection' entries refer to the books of collected, written, authenticated sayings of the Prophet Muhammad, peace and blessings upon him.

Islam is primarily an oral tradition, so aside from *hadith* (Prophetic sayings) specialists, and students studying under their guidance, these collections are not appropriate for most lay people to study. They are given here for specialists, and to reassure Muslims that the teachings in this book come from legitimate sources.

For further exploration into any of the concepts shared in the book, I recommend going through the resources and accompanying video guide at: www.InsideTheSoulOfIslam.com/Guide

Introduction

1. See the Ben Affleck video at: www.InsideTheSoulOfIslam.com/Guide

Chapter 1: What is the Soul of Islam?

1. Collection: Bukhari

Chapter 2: How I Discovered the Soul of Islam

1. Quran 2: 170
2. Collection: Daraqutni
3. Quran 2: 44
4. Collection: Tabarani

Chapter 3: Uncovering Spiritual Reality

1. Sydney Banks, *The Missing Link*, 1988
2. Collection: Bayhaqi
3. For Banks' comprehensive definitions of the Three Principles of Mind, and more resources, visit: www.InsideTheSoulOfIslam.com/Guide
4. *William James and The Varieties of Religious Experience: A centenary celebration*; edited by Jeremy Carrette Ch. 2: 'Psychologies as ontology-making practices,' Sonu Shamdasani
5. ibid.
6. Special thanks to Keith Blevens PhD for many years of rigorous compilation of these sayings, and for distilling the logic within them for our benefit. For more of Keith's teachings, visit: www.InsideTheSoulOfIslam.com/Guide
7. Sydney Banks, *The Best of Two Worlds*. For more from Sydney Banks, visit: www.InsideTheSoulOfIslam.com/Guide

Chapter 4: Quran – the Divine Revelation

1. Quran 3: 2–3
2. Collection: Tirmidhi

3. Quran 59: 23
4. Quran 95: 8
5. Quran 49: 13
6. Dalia Mogahed, John Esposito, 'Who Speaks For Islam: What a Billion Muslims Really Think,' based on Gallup Survey. Research conducted over six years, based on 50,000 interviews.
7. Quran 2: 256
8. Quran 109: 1–6
9. Quran 4: 82
10. Quran 3: 7

Chapter 5: Loving Kindness – the Starting Point

1. Quran 1: 1
2. Quran 1: 1–7
3. Collection: Muslim
4. Quran 21: 107
5. Collection: Tirmidhi
6. Collection: Ibn Majah
7. Collection: Muslim
8. Collection: Muslim
9. Collection: Ibn Asakir
10. Collection: Mishkat al-Masabih
11. Collection: Tirmidhi
12. Quran 1: 1–7

Chapter 6: Knowledge – the Path of the Seeker

1. Collection: Ibn Majah
2. Quran 96: 1–5
3. Collection: Bukhari
4. Quran 5: 16

5. Collection: Bukhari
6. Collection: Darimi
7. Collection: Al-Bukhari
8. Imam Abu Hamid al-Ghazali, *Revival of the Religious Sciences Volume 1: The Book Of Knowledge*
9. Collection: Daylami
10. Imam Abu Hamid al-Ghazali, *Revival of the Religious Sciences Volume 1: The Book Of Knowledge*
11. Collection: Tirmidhi
12. Collection: Muslim
13. Collection: Tirmidhi
14. Imam Abu Hamid al-Ghazali, *Revival of the Religious Sciences Volume 1: The Book Of Knowledge*

Chapter 7: Spreading Peace – The First Commandment

1. Collection: Ibn Majah
2. Collection: Muslim
3. Collection: Nasa'i; Ahmed
4. Quran 25: 63
5. Collection: Ahmed

Chapter 8: Presence – the Key to Paradise

1. Quran 55: 60
2. Collection: Bukhari
3. Imam Abu Hamid al-Ghazali, *Revival of the Religious Sciences, Volume 4: Secrets of Prayer*
4. Quran 2: 112
5. Quran 112: 1–4
6. Collection: Bukhari

Chapter 9: Remembrance – the Spiritual Cure

1. Quran 62: 1
2. Quran 2: 152
3. Collection: Bukhari
4. Collection: Bukhari
5. Collection: Tirmidhi
6. Quran 13: 28
7. Quran 33: 41–42
8. Quran 33: 35
9. Quran 29: 45
10. Quran 38: 87
11. Collection: Bayhaqi
12. www.theguardian.com/uk/2008/aug/20/|uksecurity.terrorism1
13. Collection: Tabarani

Chapter 10: Speaking Truth – the Highest Form of Courage

1. Quran 33: 70–71
2. Collection: Ibn al Mubarak
3. Collection: Bukhari
4. Collection: Imam Ahmed
5. Collection: Ibn Hiban
6. Quran 20: 44
7. This is a joke.
8. Quran 49: 12
9. Collection: Muslim
10. Quran 24: 15
11. Collection: Tabarani
12. Collection: Abu Dawud
13. Collection: Daylami
14. Quran 28: 55

Chapter 11: Resilience – the Greatest Virtue

1. Quran 2: 153
2. Collection: Bukhari
3. Quran 16: 127
4. Quran 40: 55
5. Collection: Muslim
6. Quran 2: 153–157
7. Quran 36: 82–83
8. Quran 2: 156
9. Collection: Tirmidhi
10. Quran 1: 1
11. Imam Abu Hamid al-Ghazali: *Revival of the Religious Sciences, Volume 40: Remembrance of Death and the Afterlife*

Chapter 12: Inspired Action – the Fruit of Belief

1. Quran 95: 4–6
2. Quran 67: 2
3. Collection: Bukhari
4. Quran 2: 177
5. Collection: Bukhari
6. Collection: Nawawi: *Riyadh as-Saliheen*
7. Collection: Bukhari
8. Collection: Daylami
9. Collection: Bukhari
10. Collection: Bukhari
11. Imam Abu Hamid al-Ghazali, *Dear Beloved Son*
12. Collection: Muslim
13. Quran 26: 88–89
14. Collection: Bukhari
15. Collection: Muslim
16. Quran 103: 1–3

Chapter 13 Gratitude – the Source of Abundance

1. Quran 31: 46
2. Collection: Bukhari
3. Collection: Bukhari
4. Quran 14: 7
5. Quran 2: 172
6. Quran 2: 152
7. Collection: Tirmidhi
8. Quran 2: 245
9. Quran 34: 39

Chapter 14: Jihad – *the Universal Human Value*

1. 'Whoever saves one innocent life, it is as if they had saved the whole of humanity.' Quran 5: 32
2. Quran 4: 75
3. The 10 Rules of War given by the Prophet, peace and blessings upon him:

   Do not kill women (Collection: Abu Dawud)

   Do not kill children (Collection: Abu Dawud)

   Do not kill civilians (Quran 2: 190; Tafsir Tabari; Collection: Ahmed); 'The most tyrannical of people to Allah the Exalted is he who kills those who did not fight him.'

   Do not kill non-combatants (Quran 2: 190; Tafsir Tabari; Collection: Ahmed); 'The most tyrannical of people to Allah the Exalted is he who kills those who did not fight him.'

   Do not kill worshippers (Collection: Ahmed)

   Do not kill the elderly (Collection: Abu Dawud)

   Do not kill the sick (Collection: Abu Dawud)

   Do not destroy villages or towns (Collection: Bukhari)

Do not cut down a tree (Collection: Muwatta)

Do not use fire (Collection: Abu Dawud)

4. Other rules:

Do not practice treachery or mutilation. (Collection: Muwatta)

Accustom yourselves to do good if people do good, and to not wrong them, even if they commit evil. (Collection: Tirmidhi)

If one fights his brother, he must avoid striking him in the face, as he was created in the image of Adam (peace and blessings upon him). (Collection: Bukhari)

5. Collection: Bayhaqi

6. To view the video of Shaykh Abdallah Bin Bayyah, and to access other resources visit: www.InsideTheSoulOfIslam.com/Guide

7. *The Covenants of the Prophet Muhammad with the Christians of the World* (Angelico Press/Sophia Perennis, 2013), Dr. John Andrew Morrow

8. Collection: Tabarani

Chapter 15: Denial – the Path of Self-Destruction

1. The Quran, A New Oxford Translation, Professor Abdul Haleem

2. Quran 2: 6–7

3. Quran 36: 54

4. Quran 6: 164

5. Quran 2: 170

6. Quran 36: 60–61

7. Quran 2: 8–10

8. Quran 2: 11–13

9. Quran 2: 256

10. Quran 109: 1–6

Chapter 16: Psychological Idolatry: the Source of Spiritual Sickness

1. Quran 2: 256–257
2. Quran 6: 108
3. Collection: Bukhari
4. Sydney Banks, *The Best of Two Worlds*. For more, see the accompanying video guide at: www.InsideTheSoulOfIslam.com/Guide
5. Quran 31: 13
6. Collection: Ahmed
7. Collection: Bukhari
8. Collection: Bukhari
9. Collection: Bukhari
10. Narrator: Abu Hurraira. For audio by Shaykh Mortada, visit: www.InsideTheSoulOfIslam.com/Guide
11. Collection: Muslim
12. Sirah: Ibn Hisham
13. Collection: Bukhari
14. Quran 2: 201
15. Shaykh Zakariya al-Siddiqi, *How to Memorize the Quran*; see www.InsideTheSoulOfIslam.com/Guide
16. Quran 3: 14–17
17. Collection: Ibn Majah
18. Collection: Muslim
19. Quran 7: 146
20. Quran 40: 35
21. Quran 23: 16
22. Collection: Muslim
23. Hamza Yusuf, *Purification of the Heart: Signs, Symptoms and Cures of the Spiritual Diseases of the Heart*

24. Collection: Ahmed
25. Collection: Tirmidhi
26. Collection: Bukhari
27. Quran 49: 12
28. Imam Abu Hamid al-Ghazali, *Revival of the Religious Sciences Volume 1: The Book Of Knowledge*

Chapter 17: Forgiveness – the Self-Healing System

1. Collection: Tirmidhi
2. Collection: Muslim
3. Collection: Tirmidhi
4. Collection: Ahmed
5. Collection: Ahmed
6. Collection: Bukhari
7. Collection: Bukhari
8. Collection: Tirmidhi
9. Collection: Bukhari
10. Collection: Bayhaqi; *Branches of Faith*
11. Ibn Ata'illah, *Hikam*
12. Collection: Bukhari

Conclusion: The Healing Power of Islam

1. Quran 13: 11
2. Quran 5: 32
3. Quran 2: 153–157
4. Ibn Ata'illah, *Hikam*
5. Imam Abu Hamid al-Ghazali, *Dear Beloved Son*

Acknowledgments

I begin by thanking Allah and His Messenger, without whom the secrets of this Path would have remained hidden from view.

A special thanks to my mother, and to my mother, and to my mother, and to my father. I hope this book lets you know that all the times I didn't call, I was doing something worthwhile, for which you will undoubtedly receive rewards and blessings, *insha'Allah.*

A thanks to the women who raised me, nurtured me, taught me, and loved me: those who did so throughout my childhood and those who continue to do so in my adulthood. You are the gems of this world, and your love keeps it from falling apart.

An enormous thanks to the Hay House team. It was in the first meeting with Michelle Pilley that the intention of Hay House was clear: to create some good karma. May Allah bless you infinitely for seeing the desperate need for this work and for giving it your platform. I ask readers to pray for the success of the Hay House team, in this life and eternally, and that they receive all the rewards possible from such a noble project.

Thank you Amy for holding me to the vision of this project, and giving much-needed encouragement along the way, and Julie for holding me to delivering it as close to 'on time' as possible for a Pakistani.

And Reid, for the advice you gave me when we first met, and for directing me to the Writer's Workshop, where it all began.

Thank you Shaykh Babikar, Shaykh Hasan al Banna, Shaykh HammadurRahman Fahim, Keith Blevens, Valda Monroe, Ustadh Abdelkadir Harkassi, Bobby Kegley, Debra Wolter, Najiba, and Rachida. This book would have been embarrassingly full of mistakes, had it not been for you reading and correcting it over and over again. For taking out precious time during the blessed month of Ramadan, may you be rewarded with bounties known only to Allah, the Most Generous.

Chantel and Team for keeping my business ticking along for months, so I could just write.

(And one more special thanks, just for the boyz.)

Index

ABOUT THE AUTHOR

Lesli Taihuttu

Mamoon Yusaf is a thought leader, peace activist, and transformational coach of the Muslim community. He is the star of the popular TV shows *The Quran Coach* and *Taqwa Transformation*, in which he changes people's lives through his powerful message of the truth of the Inside-Out paradigm.

He's the creator of the 'Quran For Busy People' blog and podcast, which has a current subscription base of over 10,000 people from all over the world. His transformational online training programs include Effortless Transformation, Quran for Busy People, Enlightened Relationships, and many more.

Mamoon is the co-founder of IMPACT (the International Membership of Professional Advisors, Coaches and Trainers) and has delivered coaching programs on behalf of some of the biggest names in the personal development industry.

He currently lives in London, but travels all over the world to deliver personal development seminars, speak about the Inside-Out Paradigm, and hang out with clients and friends.

www.insidethesoulofislam.com

We hope you enjoyed this Hay House book. If you'd like to receive our online catalog featuring additional information on Hay House books and products, or if you'd like to find out more about the Hay Foundation, please contact:

Hay House, Inc., P.O. Box 5100, Carlsbad, CA 92018-5100
(760) 431-7695 or (800) 654-5126
(760) 431-6948 (fax) or (800) 650-5115 (fax)
www.hayhouse.com® • www.hayfoundation.org

Published and distributed in Australia by:
Hay House Australia Pty. Ltd., 18/36 Ralph St., Alexandria NSW 2015
Phone: 612-9669-4299 • *Fax:* 612-9669-4144 • www.hayhouse.com.au

Published and distributed in the United Kingdom by:
Hay House UK, Ltd., Astley House, 33 Notting Hill Gate, London W11 3JQ
Phone: 44-20-3675-2450 • *Fax:* 44-20-3675-2451 • www.hayhouse.co.uk

Published and distributed in the Republic of South Africa by:
Hay House SA (Pty), Ltd., P.O. Box 990, Witkoppen 2068
info@hayhouse.co.za • www.hayhouse.co.za

Published in India by: Hay House Publishers India,
Muskaan Complex, Plot No. 3, B-2, Vasant Kunj, New Delhi 110 070
Phone: 91-11-4176-1620 • *Fax:* 91-11-4176-1630 • www.hayhouse.co.in

Distributed in Canada by:
Raincoast Books, 2440 Viking Way, Richmond, B.C. V6V 1N2
Phone: 1-800-663-5714 • *Fax:* 1-800-565-3770 • www.raincoast.com

---